THE YARN WHISPERER

C. 1

THE YARN WHISPERER

My Unexpected Life in Knitting

Clara Parkes

STC CRAFT | A MELANIE FALICK BOOK NEW YORK

FOR CLARE

Published in 2013 by Stewart, Tabori & Chang
An imprint of ABRAMS

Cataloging-in-Publication Data has been applied for and may be obtained from the Library of Congress.
ISBN: 978-1-61769-002-0

Editor: Melanie Falick
Designer: Mary Jane Callister
Production Manager: Tina Cameron

The text of this book was composed in Sentinel and Bryant.

Printed and bound in the U.S.A.
10 9 8 7 6 5 4 3 2 1
Stewart, Tabori & Chang books are available at special discounts when purchased in quantity for premiums and promotions as well as fundraising or educational use. Special editions can also be created to specification. For details, contact specialsales@abramsbooks.com or the address below.

THE ART OF BOOKS SINCE 1949

115 WEST 18TH STREET, NEW YORK, NY 10011
WWW.ABRAMSBOOKS.COM

CONTENTS

PREFACE

BEING CALLED A "knitting rock star" is like being voted the best Pakistani restaurant by the *Bangor Daily News.* It's an honor, but not the kind that'll get you a last-minute table at Le Bernardin or an order of chivalry from the Queen. No doorman has ever pulled aside the velvet cord for a famous knitter. And yet after more than a decade of hard work and persistent diligence, I find myself being labeled as such. I've been lucky.

And what does a knitting rock star look like, you ask? For starters, I intentionally reside in a town of 910, my bedtime rarely inches past 10 p.m., and my version of trashing a hotel room involves twice stealing the salt and pepper shakers from my room service tray—though, in my defense, I *did* give a generous tip.

I can swear like a sailor, but I'm a fiercely loyal friend and will do almost anything to avoid hurting someone's feelings. I haven't had a "real" day job in twelve years. I miss direct deposit and paid time off, and—oh my—how I long for that posh health insurance policy.

Since turning my life over to yarn, I've lived easily a dozen lives. It's been at times thrilling, scary, and devastating. The road has had some stunning vistas, a few steep inclines, and its share of rim-bending potholes. My inner airbags have deployed more than once. But the path has always pulled me forward. I'm fortunate, and I'm grateful.

At the bottom of it all is one simple fact: I love yarn. Ever since I can remember, yarn has enchanted me. When I first asked my grandma—my mother's mother, who has figured prominently in my knitting life—to teach me how to knit, it wasn't to make anything in particular; I wanted to know *how you made yarn work.* I knew it had energy, that I could perform a series of actions with my hands that would bring it to life. To me, seeing those skeins of yarn was like finding a book written in a foreign language; I wanted to be able to read it.

Some need to knit to be happy. They churn through yard after yard of fabric, like lawn mowers, processing thoughts and worries as they go. Or they produce garment upon garment, careful, thorough masterpieces. I'm more sporadic in my progress, more interested in the journey than the destination. But I do need yarn. For me it represents the purest essence of what is good about knitting: possibility, an open road, limitless potential. Like the soil we work and the food we eat, yarn gives life.

Years ago, I was living in San Francisco and editing a technology magazine, the contents of which I didn't really understand. I'd stumbled back into knitting after years of being away, and it was a welcome source of oxygen for my increasingly stifled mind. I discovered a yarn store not too far from my office; it was my lunchtime refuge.

My stash grew wildly by the week—yarn, needles, tools, patterns, and books. Many, many books. Most were how-to books and pattern collections. I remember one in particular called *Knitting in America*. It had patterns, but they were all far too ornate and sophisticated for my skills. What I loved about this book was that it featured people from around the country who had figured out how to do what they love. They made their living in yarn, in raising animals, in dyeing, in designing...the paths were different, but the destination was the same. I felt a kinship, as if I'd finally found my people.

Fast-forward a few years. I'd moved to Maine and was working as a freelancer, still in technology. My coworker and I were conjuring an editorial start-up of our own. It was going to be all about people who'd found their way, who were living with their grain instead of against it. I would be the writer.

My colleague fed me names and stories he thought suitable for the project. A man who'd left his family behind to sail around the world for a year. Another man who'd made a fortune in investments. A third man who raced cars.

I opened up my trusty copy of *Knitting in America* and found my own stories. I picked Margrit Lohrer and Albrecht Pichler, the founders of Morehouse Merino, successful urban dwellers who had managed to create a meaningful parallel life in the country just north of New York City. I wrote their story, borrowing so heavily from *Knitting in America* that it teetered on the edge of plagiarism. The act of telling a story that resonated with me—the physical process of running those words through my mind and out my fingers onto a keyboard, screen, and eventually paper—energized me. It was so easy and fluent, as if I were finally speaking my native tongue after years of speaking someone else's. I was home.

When I shared the story with my colleague, he replied, "I get that you like the story, but really. Sheep?"

That was all I needed to hear. I politely backed out of the project, and, just four months later, sent out the first issue of *Knitter's Review*. Every week, I'd publish thoughtful, in-depth reviews of yarns, tools, books, and events that shaped the knitting experience. That was September 2000. It's safe to say that hundreds of yarns have flowed through my fingers since then; I've met thousands of people, written millions of words.

Stories are like buildings. You see them from the outside, you see their structure and potential, you see light in the windows and want to get inside. The writer's job is to find the right door. Once you do, the rest of the journey often comes easily. I'd found that door; my adventure was a gift. Today I open the pages of *Knitting in America* and realize that, quite by chance, many of its characters have since become personal friends. The leap from icon to friend is utterly surreal.

I remember meeting Meg Swansen in 1995, at my first Stitches West event. Already on yarn overload, I rounded a corner and came to a booth filled with books. A beautiful woman stood at the table. She turned to me and smiled that twinkly, electric smile. Time stopped as my mind connected the dots and I realized Meg Swansen was standing before me—the famous teacher, designer, author, and daughter of Elizabeth Zimmermann. My heart leapt and my mouth fell open, but no words came out. Instead, I walked away as quickly as I could. Twelve years later, we were sitting together under a plum tree in Oregon after the first Sock Summit, knitting and talking. When I stripped aside all the baggage we tend to add to famous people, I was amazed to discover that I really liked Meg as a person—her wisdom, humor, vulnerability, all of it.

That's been the most amazing part about this journey—the people. My quest to find good yarns and tell their stories has brought me face-to-face with an astonishing assortment of people I would never have met otherwise: Melinda Kjarum, who raises Icelandic sheep in Minnesota (when her oldest ram, Ivan, was still alive, she would rub his arthritic joints with pennyroyal oil each evening). Eugene Wyatt, a Merino sheep farmer who plays trombone to scare away the coyotes and frequently quotes Proust in his blog. Melanie Falick, the author of *Knitting in America*, who happened to edit the very same book you now hold in your hands. My circle is complete.

The knitting world has changed dramatically since I first entered it. The doors to the establishment have blown wide open. Each person has vastly more opportunity to carve out a niche for him- or herself. We have greater transparency in terms of what we're using and where it came from. And we have greater choices than ever before.

Buying yarn is easy. A few clicks, and we can see what other people thought of it, what they knit with it, how they liked it, and how much of it they still have left in their stash. We can find dozens, if not hundreds, of suitable patterns—and we can see what other yarns people used for those patterns, what they thought of them, how *they* worked out.

Filter the chatter, block out the surrounding landscape, and you're left with one thing: yarn. Therein lies the real adventure, and the key to my own heart. A good yarn is better than any table at Le Bernardin.

In Victorian times, people often spoke through flowers. They called it *floriography*. A single acacia signified secret love, an oxeye daisy called for patience, and the pear blossom spoke of lasting friendship. But, as in Agatha Christie's Miss Marple mysteries, some were harbingers of danger, dishonesty, even death. Women "corresponded" through flowers, able to communicate far deeper meaning through them than they could put into words.

What if it turns out we do the same thing with yarn, creating swatches and garments that, when deciphered, tell stories of their own? Stockinette, ribbing, cables, even the humble yarn over can instantly evoke places, times, people, conversations—all those poignant moments we've tucked away in our memory banks. Over time, those stitches form a map of our lives.

This book is a collection of my own musings on stitches—why we work them, what they do to fabric, and how they have contributed to the fabric of my own life. For life really *is* a stitch. It has a beginning, a midpoint, and an end. It serves a purpose, and if we're lucky, it creates something beautiful and enduring.

ON FAKERY—
AND CONFIDENCE

WHEN I GRADUATED from college, I immediately got a job as a customer service representative for Macy's at the Bayfair Mall in San Leandro, California. Four years at an institution of higher learning, fluency in French, and the ability to intelligently analyze works of art were worth, as it turned out, exactly twenty cents. They offered me $6.10 per hour, but then raised it to $6.30, citing my degree as the reason.

During my two-day training, I learned how to do everything my job didn't entail, things like operating a register, cashing out, issuing a credit, and weighing myself on the scale in the women's restroom. Then my manager took me aside and reassured me that customer service was better than the other departments. This was the career track. I was *behind the counter*. Work hard and you could get ahead, she said. Look at her, she'd been working that very same desk since it opened in 1957.

My department was at the end of a hallway with a dropped ceiling, fluorescent lighting, and linoleum floors that gave a distinctly Soviet-era sense of doom. I met customers at a Formica counter in the middle of which sat a button. Press it, and an old-fashioned-doorbell *ding-dong* could be heard in back. People loved that button. One woman came in for battle about a grease-caked pressure cooker that she wanted to return although it was years old and she had no receipt. She plunked her toddler on the counter, and he pressed the button incessantly.

"Can I help you?" *Ding-dong, ding-dong.*

"Yeah, this thing doesn't work *(ding-dong)* and they won't *(ding-dong)* give me another one." *Ding-dong.*

Behind the counter, a tall divider concealed a windowless back office with several empty desks and squeaky chairs, gray metal file cabinets, and a carpet that was once tan. This was my safe haven.

I had no idea what I was doing. Not a clue. I was the destination for people who needed authoritative answers. I couldn't tell them the store hours without looking them up. Housewares? I think it's on this floor. No, wait, maybe on the first floor. I'm sorry, hold on a second, let me look that up.

The phone was always ringing. "I just bought a set of sheets and washed them, but now I've changed my mind; can I still bring them back?" How should I know? At first I took messages, trying to research the answer and call people back. But the calls didn't stop coming. I put people on hold until they hung up. The messages piled up, and eventually I started stuffing them into my purse and throwing them away when I got home. I felt like someone had put me at the helm of a nuclear submarine. No matter what button I pushed, something was going to blow up.

On Fridays, it was my job to hand out the paychecks to my fellow employees. They stood, fingers tapping, while I leaned into the special paycheck cabinet under the counter to find their envelopes. The men seemed especially eager to help me navigate the alphabet. They'd lean over the counter and peer into the box with me. "That's F... no wait, you're on E, one more ... " It took me exactly two weeks to realize they were just trying to get a better look down my shirt.

The store was always pushing credit, offering the usual "10 percent off today if you open an account with us" deal. Employees received a scratch-off game card every time someone opened an account successfully. Even I won $200, which I promptly took to the jewelry department and spent, using my employee discount, on a Movado watch.

But when someone's credit was declined—and this happened frequently—that unfortunate person was sent to me to hear the bad news. They already knew what was coming, but still they came. I could recognize the credit application as it marched toward me, clenched in someone's fist. They had no idea what could be wrong. Everything was fine. Their credit was perfect. They needed that leather sofa. "That's horrible," I'd say, feigning astonishment and indignation on their behalf. I played good cop to the credit department's bad cop. "I'm going to call those people right now and find out what's wrong."

Then I'd take the smudged, crumpled application, pick up my phone, and call the credit folks—who would proceed to tell me the real story. This guy already had three outstanding accounts with the company, all of which were in collections. He lied about his employer. He was nine months in arrears on his child support. There was a warrant out for his arrest, and I should seek shelter and call the police immediately.

My job was to listen to this information without changing my facial expression. Then I had to translate it to the person standing in front of me in such a way that he would nod and walk away instead of yelling, pleading, sobbing, or becoming physically violent. I don't have an ounce of joyful prison guard in me. I tend to voluntarily take on other people's pain and embarrassment. I felt guilty and small and horrible being the one to convey bad news to people who, more often than not, already knew it was coming. There I was, fresh from college with good credit and a job. Who was I to tell this guy he didn't deserve a new dining-room set?

But I stumbled upon a strange and liberating universal truth: Faking confidence works. The people who came to me with their dented pressure cookers and falsified credit applications? More often than not, they weren't prepared to bare their souls and walk with me, hand in hand, in pursuit of a resolution that was both just and true. No, they simply needed an answer, a definitive line in the sand, a boundary. Even if the answer was "I don't know," it needed to be presented by someone who exuded unshakable confidence. When it was, they nodded and went away. Just like that.

This was a revelation to me, but also a challenge. I wasn't raised to exude confidence. I was raised to agree, to support, and to stand out as little as possible. You may know my mother from such hits as, "What should I order?" and "Am I cold? Do I need a sweater?" Meanwhile, my father was happily tucked in the Rochester Philharmonic as second-chair oboe for more than thirty years, preferring to be eaten alive by wolves than to be singled out for a standing ovation.

Nobody taught me how to assume a position of power or authority. I can tell you how to be quietly capable, how to harbor a grudge, or how to suffer with such melodramatic martyrdom that even Meryl Streep would take notes. But stand tall and say, "Sir, you're going to have to leave or I will have security escort you out of here"—that was nowhere in my cellular makeup.

You know how it's easier to clean someone else's house than your own? Well, the same is true for emotional houses. I realized I was in a living laboratory in which nobody really knew me at all, so I could experiment at being someone else— someone who had no qualms about setting boundaries and telling people what to do. I wasn't going to stay long, so what the heck? I began to dabble in being that woman in the tidy office attire, the one whose name you never bother to remember, whose leather pumps go *clickety-clack* as she marches efficiently to and fro saying "yes" and "no." The more I dabbled in this alternate über-confident persona, the more smoothly everything began to go. It wasn't that I was blatantly lying to people, I was just behaving as if I knew *everything*.

My time at Macy's was brief. By fall I'd turned in my badge

and was on my way to France for a teaching fellowship. Fake Clara was lost in translation, and I spent the next year feeling like a dreadful impostor. But I still have the Movado watch, and I still marvel at the power of fakery.

In knitting, just as in, say, piloting that nuclear submarine, faking it is really not such a good idea. "I'll just keep going and see what happens" rarely bears tasty fruit. That is how you end up with a turtleneck through which your head cannot pass, a sock with no heel, or a submarine grounded off Antarctica when you expected to be somewhere in the Gulf of Mexico.

How ironic, then, that I'm back at a job where people ask me questions all the time. My inbox has become its own virtual knitting customer service desk filled with endless inquiries about yarns, fibers, patterns, breeds, shops, and places around the world. I try to answer each one, but they just keep coming, and sometimes, like those slips of paper, I have to admit defeat and hit the "delete" button. Some things I know; some things I don't. I try to help whenever I can.

Questions are a curious thing. Have you noticed that we often ask questions to which we've already decided the answer? We're just fishing to see if you choose the same answer we did. We don't *really* want to know what you think about the difference between Merino and alpaca, just like we don't really want to know what you think about our lousy boyfriend. No, we just want to see if you think that yellow skein would make as pretty a scarf as we do.

No matter how I answer, you'll either buy it or you won't. You'll either stay with Gary or break up with him. In fact, unless the yarn poses an immediate physical threat to you, my answer is almost irrelevant. I hope so, because the burden of making other people's decisions is too weighty for my shoulders.

When I started baking at my local café, a side gig to help me work through my apparent butter fixation, I found myself right back at the Bayfair Mall. I am not a trained chef. I'm a passionate, self-taught home baker. But all the customers saw was a person behind the counter. From day one, those old Macy's questions returned. "What's a 'milky way'?" they asked. How many shots go into a macchiato? What kind of soy milk do we use? They've handed me résumés, they've asked me to sign delivery slips, they've alerted me to a running toilet or an empty soap dispenser.

I marvel at how little a clue I have about any of it. How refreshingly terrifying. But I do remember the old routine: Stand up straight and project my ignorance in a way that instills complete confidence. People don't want to hear someone wallow in all the ways she can't help them—they want someone to nod, perhaps tell them who *can* help.

When I toggle between my days as an impostor-baker and the more comfortable ones as a knitting expert, the confidence part doesn't seem to be going away. What I'd assumed was total fakery on my part might actually be rooted in something, dare I say, genuine? Maybe the original lesson I learned at Macy's wasn't to *fake* it, like the giant fraud I felt I was, but simply to present whoever and whatever I am with confidence.

After all, did Elizabeth Zimmermann encourage us to knit on with fear and uncertainty? No. Her exact words were, "Knit on, with confidence and hope, through all crises." And so I shall.

THE THING
ABOUT BOBBLES

MY MATERNAL GRANDMA always wore turtlenecks. Not until late in life, after dementia took its toll, her long braids were lopped off, and her Icelandic sweaters replaced by wash-and-wear polyester gowns, did I discover the reason why: Her upper chest and neck were peppered with a faint, fleshy constellation of skin tags. According to my mother, · my ever-tactful grandfather felt compelled to snort at some point in the summer of 1957, "Ruth, put on a turtleneck; those things are disgusting."

From that moment on, she never left the house uncovered again. I can find no photos of her ever sporting a bathing suit, shorts, or even a short-sleeved shirt. When she came to visit us in Arizona and the temperatures hovered around 100 degrees, the turtleneck was still firmly in place, sleeves marching defensively to her tiny wrists. It was her version of a burka, protecting a Victorian modesty that concealed a painfully fragile ego. According to family lore, she even changed into her pajamas in the closet.

How funny, then, that at the same time my grandma was so carefully covering up her neck, she was furiously adding bobbles to everything she knit, like a chef gone wild with a pastry bag. Using a seemingly endless supply of off-white, worsted-weight wool procured who knows where, she adorned pillow cover after pillow cover with complex Aran patterning that featured, always, a proliferation of bobbles.

Bobbles are the skin tags of knitted fabric, wobbly nubbins that protrude and dangle, make babies hungry, invite fiddling, distract the eye, and consume acres of yarn. While skin tags may appear suddenly and when least expected, bobbles exist only when we want them to exist.

A bobble is formed by adding several stitches onto an unsuspecting stitch, working them back and forth independently from the rest of the fabric, and then binding off all but that original stitch—which then rejoins the party as if nothing had happened, only now sporting a giant hump on its back. "Who, me? Oh, must've been that second piece of cake, ha ha," it laughs nervously as it inches into the crowd. A bobble is a whispered conversation that everyone overhears, a prominent sidebar, a weekend in Las Vegas caught on tape.

As with any protruding three-dimensional object, we've developed all sorts of techniques to make a better, firmer, tighter bobble. We've learned that if you add and bind off the extra stitches in stages, row by row, you create a rounder, more robust bobble. We've discovered that if we wrap the neighboring stitches as we go along, we can give greater support to full-figured bobbles. We've found that if we work our bobbles too close together, we'll end up with an unattractive unibobble, that it's far wiser to lift and separate our bobbles with plenty of stockinette stitches. Saggy bobbles? Try twisting the stitch in the row directly above the one in which you added the bobble.

As much as I'd like to say that bobble beauty is in the eye of the creator, it's also in the eye of the beholder. And nothing beats the awkwardness of two ill-placed bobbles on a grown-up woman's sweater. No, far better to space them evenly throughout your work.

But be careful. Adding bobbles with reckless abandon can be dangerous because there's no getting rid of a bobble once it's there. You can add new ones after the fact, no problem. But you can't freeze one off a sweater, cover it with a Band-Aid, and expect it to heal. Slice a bobble off your fabric, and the surrounding stitches will quickly open into an ever-widening yawn. A bobble is there to stay, till death do you part.

Many knitters scorn bobbles with the same disdain reserved for a neighbor's barking dog or the lumbering Winnebago that refuses to pull out of the passing lane. They are fiddly and tedious to work, always hitting the "pause" button when you've just begun to gain momentum. To knit a sweater with bobbles is to tour a museum with a friend—you know the one—who insists on stopping at each painting and reading the information card, word by word. There you stand in the doorway, eager to move into the Impressionist room while she lingers among the Pre-Raphaelites, still reading the second paragraph of the third card on the fourth painting.

Even the word *bobble* doesn't bode well. It means to make a mess of something, to mishandle it. When a horse makes a misstep before a race, it's called a bobble. Likewise, an athlete bobbles when fumbling the ball. To bobble is to lose one's grip, which is what many people think you've done when you start adding bobbles to everything. I certainly thought so.

I suspect bobble mania is especially likely to afflict those people made uncomfortable by bare walls and unadorned space. For them, a sea of stockinette is like an empty windowsill with nary a seashell or figurine to keep it company. Their immediate instinct is to put something on it, and bobbles are the knitter's favorite figurine. They adorn and punctuate the three-dimensional language of stitches, they are the smack of a dot at the bottom of an exclamation point or a wad of chewing gum on the sidewalk, a fibery tumor.

I was rather indifferent to bobbles, until the day I spotted The Jacket. Knit in bulky yarn, it had a shockingly deep collar of bobbles matched by an equally substantial swath along both cuffs in a charmingly 1960s Jackie O style. I was mesmerized. These bobbles were not discreet or subtle, they were loud, proud Dolly Parton bobbles stomping their feet on every available inch of fabric. They created a honeycomb of stitches filled with a plush, fibery sweetness I found simply irresistible.

Suddenly, and against all my better judgment, I felt a desire stir deep within my knitting loins: a desire to cast on and create this coat for my very own self. Could I, in knitting this veritable bobblepalooza, transform an eyesore into an attraction? Could I make peace with bobbles? I had to try.

The recommended yardage alone told me I was in for a long trip. You'd normally need about 840 yards to complete a comparably sized and shaped coat—and that's using a thick, bulky yarn. But this baby was asking for 1,200 yards, maybe even more. I ordered 1,400 yards of a plush, full-bodied wool yarn, figuring I could always use the extra for a matching bobbled hat and mitts. (When in Rome…)

I cast on at the bottom and worked my way up. The pattern has you add raglan-style sleeve shaping and then—only at the very end—top it all off with a heaping helping of bobbles. Progress on the body was fast as my needles cranked out sheets of bulky stockinette.

Just as I caught myself thinking, "I should have this done by the end of the weekend," I hit the bobbles. They say that driving in Africa has two extremes—one minute you're speeding along on smooth, new tarmac, and the next minute the pavement ends and you're dodging potholes big enough to swallow a Jeep. After cruising along in my smooth stockinette, I was now in first gear wondering if I'd make it to the next town by sunset.

Then something happened. A switch in my impatient brain clicked off. I stopped focusing on time and speed; I stopped anticipating the next row and the row after that. I settled into the deeper, slower pleasure of the moment and of each stitch. I savored the experience of watching that rounded shape begin and grow and finally mature into a full-bodied bobble. I became excited when it was time to bring each new bobble home to meet the family. I loved watching how the other stitches adjusted to the newcomer, and I felt almost giddy as the slow, steady body of bobbles unfolded on my needles.

I felt a sense of solidarity with my grandma, with all those bobble knitters who'd come before me. They'd stumbled upon this secret and guarded it so well. They'd endured the sneers and eye rolls of anti-bobblers, blithely continuing on their merry way. Now I understood.

I love my bobble coat more than just about anything else I've ever knit. I'm not sure it's the most flattering of garments. But when I wear it, I can quickly spot the bobble haters in the crowd and connect with the bobble sisterhood and brotherhood, those who know the secret. I love how the collar feels, and I love how it adorns and protects a neck that is beginning to sprout its own, far smaller constellation of skin tags.

Speaking of which, last week I went to the dermatologist for my annual checkup. She looked at my freckles, she measured the creepy mole on my back, and then she glanced at my neck.

"We can freeze these off if they ever start to bother you," she said.

I considered it for a moment. I thought of my grandma and her turtlenecks, and of how readily she could've had her own skin tags removed. Yet she didn't.

"You know what?" I replied, "I'm good, thanks."

A GOOD STEEK

WHEN I WAS eight years old, I came home from school one day to discover everything in my house on Bittersweet Road in Rochester, New York, had been packed and taken away, and that I was to be trundled into a car pointed west—far, far west— with only one parent coming along for the journey.

If this story had a soundtrack, here's where you'd hear a needle being yanked off a record. We met my father at a park, and my brothers and I said good-bye while my mother sat in the car. Then we drove away. Simple as that.

For my mother, it was the beginning of a glorious new life of sunshine and self-discovery. For me, propped in the back of an un-air-conditioned car with a spider plant, a Sony TV, and sullen brothers for company, this was my first real exposure to emotions beyond the realm of dropped ice cream cones or a broken toy. My heart hadn't grown a callus nearly thick enough to protect it from what was happening.

As the car continued to pull us farther and farther away from home, I couldn't help but also be curious about what I saw out my window. New things. An indoor/outdoor pool at a Holiday Inn in Illinois, the Mississippi River, a real palm tree, a hotel lounge with a live band playing "You Are the Sunshine of My Life," where I was allowed to order ginger ale for the first time.

Onward we went through the sweltering heat and increasingly barren landscape. With each state we crossed, my mother grew more jubilant, my brothers and I more impatient. I remember being hot and uncomfortable. The Instamatic camera I left in the back window melted by the time we reached Texas. Tucson was our final destination.

This was not the Tucson of today, with its multistoried resort homes, splendid golf courses, and outdoor shopping malls with fire pits, air-conditioning, gelato, and Tiffany's. It was a dry, flat place best remembered with the silence and faded colors of a Super 8 home movie.

We arrived at dusk and checked into a Howard Johnson off Interstate 10. The air smelled sweet, and a green, spiked thing was growing in a pile of rocks by the parking lot. It fascinated me. The soft fuzz between the thorns felt just like the surface of a peach. That evening I learned my first lesson of the desert: Never pet a cactus, no matter how soft it looks. It took days to pick all the tiny thorns out of my fingers. Welcome to Arizona.

Of course, my mother reminds me that we all knew about the move for months, that I even helped with some of the packing. She also points out that we left on an August morning, *not* suddenly one day after school. Rationally, I know this to be true. But my eight-year-old brain still remembers the whole experience quite differently; no amount of preparation would've changed this.

Cut something apart, and there's always a momentary shock to the system. What was once whole is now sundered. Slice through the veins of your knitted fabric, and the newly exposed stitches may easily unravel as they scramble back toward a home that no longer exists. At the same time, there's no doubting the sense of possibility that accompanies this opening, a curiosity about what the new fabric may hold.

There's a way to do it right, without pain. We work a series of steps called a steek, so that the stitches are prepared for what's coming and can absorb the shock, heal without any scars, and even thrive in their new environment. According to Alice Starmore, *steek* is an Old Scots word for hardening a heart or closing a gate—a fitting way to describe what you're doing to get those stitches ready for what *could* be a traumatic experience. Even now, I keep discovering stray loose ends from that shocking cut when I was eight years old. A favorite cup will get broken, a pen thrown away by accident, some unexpected change is foisted upon me, and I am overcome with a powerful panic I know is not rooted in the present.

A good steek is much more than just going at it with scissors. It begins at the cast-on, when you add several extra "waste" stitches to buffer each side of the cut and prevent deeper fabric erosion. Right before cutting, you'll use a sewing machine or crochet stitches to reinforce either side of the waste stitches. Secure those edges well enough, and the floodwaters will never breach. In fact, once those first steps have been taken, the cutting is almost anticlimactic. Instead of grieving the cut, your fabric can enjoy the new scenery.

We like steeks because they let us make colorful, intricate Fair Isle garments in the round without ever having to fuss with a purl row. We can just set the engine on "knit" and speed on down the road, going around and around until we're done. Then, simply pop the steek, sprout the armhole, and you're nearing the finish line before you know it. Forget to add a steek, and your sweater remains, at best, a fancy pillowcase.

Steeks represent a necessary part of life, almost a coming-of-age for fabric. As roses need pruning and seedlings need thinning, steeks require cutting if your fabric has any hope to grow into something else. Eventually, we all need to cut open our stitches to leave home and become independent human beings.

By my late twenties, I became aware that my life was calling for a steek. I'd been going around and around at a job in San Francisco. I had a cool title on an impressive-looking business card. I'd made a snazzy fabric, but it wasn't very well tailored to *me*. Either I would stay in that tube forever, my movement slowly shrinking and changing to fit the confines of the fabric, or I would do the scary thing and cut open those stitches to see what could grow.

My steek required a cross-country move back East to the scene of my childhood summers in Maine. There were two of us now. My partner, Clare, and I were knitting this new fabric together. It took us three years to build up a wide enough band of metaphorical "waste" stitches to absorb that cut and buffer us from its impact. Unlike the last time I'd gotten into a car and headed to a new home on the other coast, this time I was in the driver's seat.

On the morning of April 30, 1998, we locked the door of our apartment and handed the keys to our landlord. We got into the car—its windows sparkling clean, oil freshly changed, tires rotated, and tank full of gas—and I put the key in the ignition, took a deep breath, and squeezed the scissors.

The cut itself took almost a month to complete. We took time along the way to visit people and places that had been instrumental in the stitches of our lives. Each had a turn at the scissors. We arrived in Maine on the eve of my twenty-ninth birthday, steek fully cut, feeling exhilarated and exhausted. The heat had been turned off for the summer and our apartment was freezing—or maybe it was my own exposed inner fabric that brought the chill.

It took several months before all the ends were darned. Over the years, my colorway and pattern have changed some. I've frogged a few things and sprouted a few more openings, but the fundamental fabric holds strong—and it continues to evolve as I do. Who knows? One day we may load up the car again and head west, back to the land of palm trees, melted cameras, and abundant sunshine. Or perhaps we'll point our jalopy in an entirely new direction, carefully cut a new steek, and see what comes next. The important thing is that, now, the scissors are in *my* hands.

CHOREOGRAPHY
OF STITCHES

THREE THINGS SUM up my first few years in Tucson:
the ramada, the rodeo, and square dancing. On my
first day at Peter E. Howell Elementary School, we
were told to gather under the ramada after recess.
The what? I came from a place with seasons, where
you had to play indoors roughly half of the school
year. Here in the land of eternal sunshine, on a playground that resembled the moon, they had put a
flat roof on metal posts over a rectangular slab of
concrete. This was the only place you could go to
escape the sun—and it was, as I learned that first
day, called a *ramada.*

Tucson also brought me the rodeo. Until then,
the only rodeo I knew was the ballet scored by Aaron
Copland and choreographed by Agnes de Mille,
which I'd seen performed by the American Ballet
Theatre the year we left New York. While my

father played in the orchestra pit, my best friend, Carol, and I watched from front-row seats. At intermission, I led her out a secret door—the Eastman Theatre was my playground back then—but it locked behind us. We were stuck in a small vestibule with two other locked doors. We pounded on all of them until one opened, revealing the magical world of backstage.

The stage manager—who knew my father—ushered us inside. The only way back into the theater was through a door on the other side of the stage, he explained, and we couldn't walk behind the stage because intermission was almost over. He offered us something even better: We got to stand in the eaves, just out of view of the audience, and watch the rest of the ballet from there. I remember stunningly beautiful dancers standing in what looked like adult-sized litter boxes rubbing their toes in the sand, staring fixedly at the stage, then suddenly sprinting out of their boxes and back on the stage, their mouths flashing into toothy smiles. That's what I thought of when I heard the word *rodeo*.

But Tucson's version was nothing like the world of Copland and de Mille. It was hot, loud, and dusty. We sat in crowded bleachers that were sticky and smelled of beer. A man's voice droned over the loudspeakers like a buzzing fly, incomprehensible. Somewhere in the middle of the dust and clouds, people were doing things on horses. I think I saw a cow or two, or was that what they called a bull? I didn't know.

The clown was unlike any of the happy, Technicolor Ronald McDonald circus clowns I'd ever seen. This one was dusty. He'd fallen on hard times. I imagined he lived on freight trains and ate bits of rattlesnake he'd roasted on a stick over the campfire. He did crazy things and was constantly ducking into a barrel to avoid being trampled, and people applauded it.

Arizona had only been a state for sixty-four years at this point, and the Wild West spirit still reigned. We even had a formal school holiday—"rodeo vacation"—so that we could all hitch our wagons and head out to the fairgrounds for some roping and cattle rustling.

How I longed for my gorgeous dancers trotting in their sandboxes, for the creaky wood floors of the Botsford School of Dance and the piano player who accompanied us as we flailed around, dreaming we were prima ballerinas. I missed being able to run around barefoot on the grass. I longed for tall, leafy trees and soft snow and my father in his blue cashmere sweater.

Then came square dancing, which I soon discovered was as important a school ritual as math, science, or the daily recital of the Pledge of Allegiance. Every week we'd file down to the cafeteria, line up, and march to the yammering orders and old-timey jingle-jangle coming from a small portable record player by the stage. "Hemmina hemmina hemmina," the man would babble, occasionally calling us to "allemande left, chase yer neighbor, do-si-do" before resuming the random "hemmina hemmina hemmina...". We'd march to and fro in clunky synchronization like awkward little Maoist soldiers.

After the initial affront, something strange clicked inside of me. The pleasant mathematical order of things overtook any of my angst about boys, breasts, or body odor. I liked how all our movements fit together like clockwork. There was nothing per-

sonal about this. I wasn't waiting for a boy to ask me to dance—
we all had to do-si-do, no matter what, or the engine would
come to a stop. Each person played a vital role in keeping the
machine running smoothly.

This may be part of why I like knitting so much. All knitting
is choreography. Some moves are more graceful than others,
but they all fit together and create one cohesive piece of fabric.
Whether it's an allemande left or a simple pirouette, each move
dictates the dance as each stitch dictates the knitting. Both
rely on discrete elements that are arranged and repeated in a
certain fashion, whether through the movement of body alone
or that of yarn, needles, and hands. Break out into the Charles-
ton in the middle of a tango, or feather and fan in the midst of a
heavy cabled sweater, and the public will take notice.

I've always thought that ribbing was the perfect knitted
embodiment of tap dance. Knit a front-facing stitch and purl a
back-facing stitch, and you're performing a perfect shuffle ball-
change. Vary the order of your knits and purls from row to row,
and the shuffle ball-change becomes a more nuanced time-step.

Cables add the sideways shuffling of Bob Fosse, with his
telltale one-leg-behind-the-other stance and jazz hands flashing midair. Elaborate lace motifs, those are as close as we'll
ever get to classic ballet, to knitting *Swan Lake* on our needles.
Feather and fan is the ballerina seated on stage, legs straight
ahead, who opens her arms to the sky and then gracefully col-
lapses forward until she and her legs are one, the breathing
motion of yarn overs collapsing into the condensed silence of
knit two togethers.

And the truly expressive, Martha Graham–style modern dance? That likely gets you Kaffe Fassett colorwork or a particularly vibrant piece of freeform knitting, the unexpected geometry of Norah Gaughan's designs, a Cat Bordhi moebius.

In the world of knitted choreography, one stitch makes me particularly happy: the three-needle bind-off. You do this when you have two rows of live stitches you want to join conspicuously—say, you'd like to attach the front and back shoulders of a sweater and want the prominent look of a raised seam.

It begins with a lining up of the two needles, the rows of stitches facing one another. One by one, a stitch from each needle marches forward to join its partner. The two are knit together into a stitch on the right needle. Another pair joins hands and moves to the right needle, at which point the first joined pair leapfrogs over that second pair and off the fabric. On and on they go, forming an orderly line of bound-off stitches.

Every time I do this, I'm taken back to the cafeteria of Peter E. Howell. I'm wearing white painter pants, blue Adidas shoes, and my favorite blue plaid shirt with gold threads woven in and faux-pearl snaps for buttons. I've adjusted to my strange new life. My father hasn't remarried, both sets of grandparents are still alive, and I don't yet know how the story will unfold. I'm simply standing in a row eagerly waiting my turn to walk to the center, grab hands with my partner, and sashay down the line.

NOBODY'S FOOL

RIGHT AFTER I was born, my father called my Great-Aunt Kay from the hospital to tell her the news. He called collect, and she was so insulted that she refused the charges.

So heavy was the burden of her guilt that, for my sixth birthday, she made amends by shipping her mother's entire bedroom set to me. Which is just what every six-year-old girl wants, isn't it? A heavy, carved-walnut seven-piece Victorian bedroom set?

My room wasn't nearly big enough to contain it all. I was entrusted instead with just the bed, the shorter of the two dressers, and the dressing table—a real-live dressing table at which I sat, throughout my entire adolescence, and stared at myself. I looked nothing like the girls in *Seventeen* magazine. My room was nothing like their rooms, and my life, well, I might as well have been on a different planet.

But still I sat at that dressing table with my Maybelline mascara and my little tub of purple eye shadow—it had fine silver sparkles in it—carefully applying them and wishing they could somehow magically make me fit in.

By the end of college, I'd abandoned makeup entirely, dismissing it as the oppressive mantle of the patriarchy.

Then, in 2009, I got an email. Interweave was filming segments for its TV show during the National Needlework Association conference in Ohio. They wanted to do a "wild about wool" show, and would I like to host it? Sure, I said. I can prattle about wool for hours, cameras or no cameras.

Everything was fine until the producer emailed me the guidelines for being on the show. There in black and white, right below "get a professional manicure," were the dreaded words "apply your own camera-ready makeup."

The notion of talking to a potential audience of millions didn't scare me a bit. But the prospect of applying my own makeup? Terrifying. That tub of sparkly purple eye shadow had been gone for easily twenty years. I had nothing. They might as well have been asking me to hang drywall or remove an appendix.

I picked the fanciest hair salon in town, a hoity-toity place that offered sparkling water in wineglasses and advertised massages on the third floor, Botox on the fourth. I scheduled a makeup class. "Can I also schedule a manicure?" I found myself asking. How foreign were these words. Who are you, mouth, and what have you done with Clara?

Soon I was at the reception desk giving my name to a slender woman with perfect teeth and impossibly tall shoes. She tottered us to an area that resembled a giant church organ, only instead of keys and buttons and knobs it had tier upon tier of tubes and jars and bottles of color, color, and more color, stacked as high as the eye could see. (Which wasn't that high considering I'm only five foot two, but still.) A young woman swung around and smiled. I immediately forgot her name, but it ended with an "eeee" sound. We said our hellos and she glanced around me expectantly I realized she was looking for the gawky preteen daughter I'd presumably brought for the lesson

"Uh, no," I explained, "this is for me."

And we were off. She pulled my hair back and started rubbing my face with a cool gel that tingled. "I'm just applying a toner to make sure we get rid of any residual makeup."

"No worries there," I mumbled.

For almost an hour, I sat while she slathered, smeared, dotted, brushed, and blotted my face with layer upon layer of cream, paste, powder, and gel. She played a cruel trick of applying things on just one side of my face, then making me apply them on the other side. Soon I looked like a Raggedy Ann doll that had suffered a stroke. She kept notes of what she'd done, marking swirls and slashes on a drawing of a face and then adding product names and colors. The eyes alone had twelve different notations.

While I gazed at the weird face in the mirror, she asked if I felt confident enough to do this on my own.

"I think so," I lied.

"Should I start setting you up with some product?" she asked.

"Uh...sure."

The initial tab came in at $600. We slowly whittled away at her masterpiece until I left with just an etching of a face. It was still wildly over budget, but what could I do? This was television, after all.

The morning of the shoot, I met a friend at the hotel elevator. She studied my face for a good long time. "You look," she said finally, "like someone who got a very good night's rest." I decided she meant it as a compliment, but as soon as the taping was over, I returned to my room and used a hot towel to remove the well-rested face and let the puffy, jet-lagged one back out. On the washcloth was a clear outline of my face, like the Shroud of Turin.

The closest thing we have to cosmetology in the knitting world would have to be duplicate stitch. While the rest of what we do involves building our foundation from scratch, block by block, stitch by stitch, duplicate stitch is about etching new colors and fibers directly on top of existing ones. You may know it by its raised-pinkie name, Swiss darning. The goal is to trace the exact outline of the existing stitch with new yarn so that it is, in fact, a duplicate. But just like my TV-ready face, everybody knows that something is different.

The knitting show wasn't actually my first time on TV. In the 1980s, around the same time that duplicate stitch was being used on sweaters with giant shoulder pads, I appeared in a local-access TV show called *Back Alley's*. High school friends and I wrote, acted, directed, produced, filmed, and edited this path-breaking drama whose only real claim to fame was a guest appearance by the late Michael Landon. I played Alley, the wisecracking owner of the bar where all the characters hung out—when they weren't being hit on the head by watermelons and feigning amnesia in the hospital.

This led to an equally brief but illustrious career in television voice-overs that lasted, if my memory serves me right, exactly one commercial. I went into the dark, padded sound room of a Tucson studio and donned my headphones, each the size of a sweet roll. I gazed at my on-screen subject, a woman handing a bag to a customer and saying the words "thank you." That was my canvas.

I wanted this to be utterly seamless, so I got to work. What was her motivation? Did she like her job? Was this at the beginning or end of her shift? Had she eaten lunch yet? I looked closer. There was something in her expression . . . perhaps she and this man had been lovers years ago, and she was hoping he wouldn't remember—yet was secretly hurt that he didn't.

We recorded about thirty takes before the job was done. I tried to make my addition as smooth as possible, but I'm sure my voice, like even the most expertly worked duplicate stitch, still formed a slight bump on the scene's otherwise smooth surface.

That's how duplicate stitch works. It's the voice-over of the knitting world, a kind of lipstick or wig, press-on nails, a fresh coat of paint. Anything bigger and you're asking for trouble.

Not too long after we moved to Tucson, my brothers and I witnessed a failed duplicate stitch attempt. Both my parents had begun sowing their wild oats after the divorce was declared final. My mother dated an assortment of fellows, musicians and astronomers and waiters alike. My father soon fell in love with one of his college students. They made plans to marry, but there was a slight problem. She belonged to a church that didn't believe in divorce.

For the new marriage to take place at the church, my parents' marriage had to be declared null and void—not just from that day forward, but as in "never legitimately happened." So everyone filled out a heap of paperwork, answered a lot of nosy questions, and mailed in their checks. In return, the church pulled out its giant magic darning needle, threaded it with a particularly bright white acrylic, and proceeded to cover my legitmate childhood with shiny new pretend stitches.

Of course, the new stitches were perfectly obvious to everyone, like the clumsy detective wearing dark glasses and a false mustache and hiding behind a potted palm. I was unimpressed. But it was enough for the Powers that Be. History annulled, the marriage was allowed to proceed.

Today I live in my Great-Aunt Kay's old farmhouse, and I still have that bedroom set. Now instead of pimples and adolescent angst, the mirror reflects fading hair pigment and strange creases where once my skin was smooth. I can see the temptation to start dubbing, spreading thick coats of spackling compound over the cracks.

But it never works. I consider the lovely women at my hoity-toity salon, with their biologically implausible hair colors and faces stapled open in expressions of perpetual surprise. Or my TV-ready face, or even that white acrylic lump of duplicate stitches on my childhood fabric. We're not fooling anyone.

HOW DOES YOUR GARDEN GROW?

GARDENING IS THE ultimate act of optimism. We plant, tend, weed, water, and wait, hoping that something beautiful will grow. Sometimes it does, sometimes it does not. The gardener learns to be philosophical.

So it is with yarn. Knitters are avid yarn gardeners, one and all. We have the formal French style of gardening, in which our yarns are neatly organized into shapely bins and boxes. Tidiness and order reign supreme. We might even have our entire stash in a database for easy reference.

The more rumpled British style of gardening has its mossy overgrown paths, the jumbled hedgerow heaps of balls and hanks, the weathered baskets that look as if they've been there forever.

And then we have the Japanese "natural farming" system of Masanobu Fukuoka, which espouses no plowing or tilling, no fertilizers, no weeding, no pesticides, no herbicides, not even any pruning. He preferred to let the vegetables find their own way—the yarn equivalent would be a skein taking up residence under the couch cushions, behind the muffin tins, or inside the piano.

A healthy yarn garden contains a broad spectrum of plants—annuals and perennials, deciduous and coniferous, rootstock and tubers alike. Most of us get our yarn as seedlings from the yarn-garden store, preferring ready-to-plant skeins, hanks, and balls. But some, the hearty back-to-the-lamb hand-spinners among us, prefer to raise their yarn from seed. They love the parental feeling of overseeing each moment of the yarn's growth, from its beginnings as wee fibers to its maturity as a fully grown skein and, ultimately, a finished garment.

Annuals are a thrill, those short-run, limited-availability skeins that only last one season and then are gone forever. Stock up! Get extra! You never know if you'll see this variety again. Such yarns give us a chance to replant, replenish, and re-envision our yarn gardens from year to year.

But others take a more practical approach, basing their yarn gardens on a foundation of hearty perennials that have the potential to bloom year after year. They pack their stashes with the stalwart tried-and-true yarns, the Brown Sheeps and Cascade 220s that we hope will be available, in some form, forever.

Stashes, like gardens, can hold surprises. My grandma's certainly did. As the resident knitter of the family, I inherited all her yarn, which she'd stored in a steamer trunk bearing her maiden initials, RL, painted in red on the side.

You could track her life through these yarns. There were inexpensive baby yarns used to clothe my mother. A bundle of light-blue cashmere dumplings bought in London after the war was over and things were looking up. A paper bag of rustic, deep blue wool labeled in pencil scrawl, "Brooksville wool," bought in my very town years ago when it had a yarn store. There are several cakes of lopi procured in Iceland during an early trip that marked a pivotal change in her knitting output, and after which she clothed me and my brothers in lopi sweaters. Finally, there were the annuals, several nameless, label-less, utterly extraordinary skeins of loosely twisted three-ply yarn in varying shades of browns and tans. I'm guessing it's some kind of alpaca blend purchased on a trip with my grandfather to South America in the 1950s to see a solar eclipse, during which their airplane lost its engine while flying over the Amazon.

So, too, can gardens tell stories and hold secrets that lay dormant for years, popping up when we least expect them. Some vigorous pruning to the family farmhouse rugosas this spring revealed not one but two peonies and a shocking red poppy, none of which I, my brothers, or even my mother remembers seeing before. They were likely planted by my great-grandmother more than seventy years ago. She died soon after I was born, but her garden still gives me gifts and surprises.

As hard as it is to say, I should point out that a healthy stash requires frequent and prudent weeding. It can easily get overrun before we notice what's happening—like the hearty white phlox that suddenly overtook my bright purple physostesia and, eventually, the entire garden path. One trip to Northhampton, Massachusetts, to the back room of WEBS, where overstocks and closeouts are piled high on warehouse shelves, and suddenly my stash is off-kilter with far too much dark purple angora, two bags of which I was morally obligated to buy because each skein had been marked down from $18 to $4. (Good, I see you agree.)

Weeding is not easy. How agonizing to yank a healthy seedling from its home and toss it on a compost pile to die a slow and painful death. I'm a bad weeder, and my garden suffers for it. As I try to find homes for the seedlings I cannot host anymore, so too do I try to find homes for the yarns that have overstayed their welcome. One person's excess is another's treasure, and we all take part in the game. We have stash swaps, we list our extra yarns online, the electronic version of setting them out in the proverbial wheelbarrows by the road, filled with daylilies marked "Free." We'll do anything rather than throw them away. Nature's improbable (and unpredictable) survival rate encourages us to buy more plants than we need, knowing that some will not make it. The same goes for yarn. In order for us to have what we need, we must stock more than we can actually use.

And then, when we least expect it, disaster strikes. We harvest a skein and notice the crumbly translucent shell of an emergent larva. Moths. Like aphids in a greenhouse, once the moths arrive, the prudent yarn gardener will spring into action. Each skein must be pulled out into the sunshine, aired, and inspected for damage.

Yarn gardens can also be plagued by bigger pests, like my toddler niece who discovered scissors and yarn at the same time. She had the same effect on that Noro Kureyon as the groundhog I once watched rear up on its hind legs, grab a tall echinacea spike, and shove the entire bloom in his mouth. *Crunch crunch crunch.*

I found his hole and guiltily flooded it with water, but still he came. I poured two bottles of cayenne pepper around the perimeter of his hole, but still he came. The only way to get rid of these pests is to bodily remove them—lifting the child from the yarn and placing her safely on the porch with a firm scolding, snaring the groundhog in a Havahart trap and taking him on an unexpected road trip.

Plants are a responsibility. The temptation to overcommit is great. In the summer months, Clare and I go into town on Saturday morning to get our sweet rolls and visit the local garden store—conveniently at the same place. Each and every Saturday, we tell ourselves, "We're not going to get more than we can plant." We look at each other. "Right?" Yes, I nod. She nods. Off we go.

An hour later, we're pulling back into the driveway with a trunk full of plants. Just this little six-pack of petunias, I say. Just a few more basil plants, she mumbles, you know, for the pesto. I'm no better at yarn stores. Just these two balls of Kidsilk Haze for a last-minute scarf. See how pretty their colors look next to one another?

After we bring them home, plants need to be put in the ground pretty quickly. Yarn, on the other hand, can remain in limbo almost indefinitely. The deeper it is shelved, the less visible its impatience. There it sits, silent, bitterly resentful that the best years of its life are being wasted in some dark, abandoned corner, or, worse yet, in a plastic tub. "I'm cashmere, for God's sake," it grumbles. "I deserve better than Rubbermaid."

Bulbs hold a particular poignancy. I remember E. B. White writing about his wife—the esteemed editor Katharine White—choosing and planting bulbs each fall. It was a yearly ritual, and neither of them could fathom not doing it, but when her health began to fail, he didn't know if she would live to see the bulbs bloom. Yet she still dreamed, ordered, and planted, because that is what we do. We tuck bulbs away into the darkness for a long winter's nap. We forget about them until spring, then we glance out at that bare patch of soil and wonder . . . did they survive? Will there be life? Like bulbs, we bury balls of yarn deep in our stashes, knowing that some day we'll wander through our garden with an empty basket and pluck them from the soil. Better yet, maybe they'll take on a life of their own, sprout little arms from which hands will grow, grab needles, and knit themselves when we aren't looking.

But they don't, and therein lies the problem with yarn stashing that does not exist in gardening. Whereas plants take care of things with minimal interference from us, yarn needs us for each stitch of its growth. Yarn won't knit itself.

Sometimes it may take a while, like the dogwood in my backyard. It was a tiny stick of a seedling in my Aunt Judy's Michigan yard when she dug it up, plopped it in a blueberry container, and gave it to me for good luck as Clare and I made our journey east to Maine from California so many years ago.

How I nurtured that little seedling, first on an apartment

windowsill, then in temporary soil, and finally planted, three years later, outside my kitchen window, where it grows now. For years I surrounded it with stakes and red tape to keep anyone from stepping on it or mowing over it accidentally. I went out and watered it, sat next to it, talked to it, for years and years—like the Alice Starmore sweater I pick up every few months and lovingly add a row or two to before tucking it away again. I began to notice the branches getting bigger. More branches grew, and one year a bird alighted on one. Then another. And last year—thirteen years to the month when Aunt Judy dug it from her garden—my little dogwood bloomed for the first time.

Seeds lose their potency after a year or two and need to be thrown away, but yarn never does. It remains tucked away right where we put it, still holding every ounce of the allure and potential that inspired us to bring it home in the first place. We owe it to our yarn to do right by it. To acquire prudently, to tend lovingly. To weed and prune judiciously, and every day, to visit it and tell it just how much we love it.

That Alice Starmore project still isn't finished, but my dogwood tells me to be patient. "Love it like you loved me," it says, "and one day it will be a sweater." When that moment comes, each stitch of the journey will have been worth it.

PUBLIC / PRIVATE

I LOVE TO travel by train. On the Amtrak Down-
easter from Portland to Boston, the tracks take you
through all sorts of unexpected places. They run
behind warehouses, salt marshes, and abandoned
amusement parks, snaking through neighborhoods
and an intimate backyard world of clotheslines,
lonely bicycles, swimming pools, and tree houses.
If you're lucky, you might even catch a child's
birthday party in progress. We all have our public
side, the tidy exterior where everything's properly
brushed, ironed, waxed, polished, tucked in, and
silky smooth with a bright white smile. And then
we have our private side, usually concealed behind
walls and gates. There we reveal a more vulnerable and intimate part of ourselves.

In the beginning, everything is equal. Most of us
start out knitting with garter stitch, working the

same knit stitch over and over again to create a fabric that looks the same on all sides. The minute we advance from garter stitch to stockinette, our knitting takes on a strange new notion of "public" and "private." What was once totally reversible fabric now has two distinctly different sides. Patterns refer to the smooth side that normally faces the world as the "right" side; the bumpy, inward-facing side is more ominously called the "wrong" side. We try to soften the blow by abbreviating these as RS and WS, but the words are still right there under the surface. What constitutes the public side and the private one? Sometimes it's in the eye of the beholder. Witness reverse stockinette stitch, which is nothing more than stockinette turned inside out.

I know some people whose private side is always exposed to the world. They're a walking vulnerability, weeping at the drop of a hat, revealing far more than is appropriate for the person or occasion. "How are you?" is usually met with a litany of problems and complaints and awkwardly personal details. I've been there myself a few times. It's as if we wandered out into the world with our sweaters on inside out by mistake.

Then there are those whose smooth public-facing side is all you or I—or maybe even they—ever see. So orderly are their stitches, so tightly held in place is their spotless, wrinkle-less, pill-free perfection, I sometimes worry that one wrong glance, one false turn, one dropped stitch and their very fabric will unravel. That's when neighbors find themselves suddenly on the evening news saying, "He seemed like such a nice guy."

Most of us learn how to knit first, so knitting becomes our

native stitch, and purling, alas, feels awkward and foreign, like trying to write with your nondominant hand. By the time I was ready to purl and make legitimate stockinette fabric, my knitting grandma had forgotten how to do it, so she couldn't teach me. I looked at pictures and figured it out for myself, but I was never entirely confident of my technique.

By comparison, the knit rows were so comfortable. I loved seeing all those happy Vs, like a row of sunbathers, a chorus line midkick, knowing that I had nothing but a smooth, easy row ahead. But the purl side? With those big purly butts and the needle tips pointing menacingly inward toward my heart? No. I always dreaded my purl rows. They were something to be rushed through, a dark forest at night, in order to reach the comforting safety of the next knit row.

Purling is the introvert stitch. It requires that you focus on *you*, looking inward instead of outward. The smooth face is gone and you see the lumps, the underbelly of your fabric, that noisy fluorescent kitchen of your favorite restaurant instead of the quiet dining room with its gently glowing candles.

Technically speaking, I have no excuse for disliking purling. I hold the yarn in my left hand, which makes my purls speedy and graceful. The yarn is already where it needs to be; I just flick my finger and up it goes onto the needle. If I were to hold the yarn with my right hand, I'd have to cross two lanes of busy stitch traffic every time I wanted to get the yarn onto that needle.

When we switch from purls to knits, our tension can change ever so slightly. If you've ever looked at a big stockinette garment and noticed it has almost a striped look to it, one row of

thick stitches and one row of thin, that's what you're seeing—
the difference in tension. I've heard people call this phenom-
enon "rowing out."

The only way to avoid rowing out, says knitting writer
and humorist Stephanie Pearl-McPhee, is to knit in the lever
style, which happens to be her technique. With the right needle
tucked under your armpit for support, your left hand maneu-
vers all the stitches into place so that your right hand can flip
over and back, over and back, forming each new loop like an
efficient factory machine. Lever knitting remains the preferred
style for production knitters who need to churn out garment
after garment as quickly as possible.

If I really concentrate, I can keep my stitches even on purl
and knit rows alike. But where's the fun in that? Why not relax
and just knit the knit rows and purl the purl rows as your
hands want to express them? The faint difference in row height
appears to me like a pulse, the tick-tock of time, breathing out
and breathing in—the essence of what it means to be a hand-
knit fabric versus one made entirely by machine.

Over the years, my relationship with the purl stitch has
evolved. What was once an inevitable means to a stockinette
end isn't all that bad now. I rather like holding the yarn close to
my heart. And I like how those purl ridges look, like hard-won
battle scars, proof of the many rows I've knit in this life.

These are the lines, cracks, and ridges we display with
pride. But what about those we prefer to keep hidden. It used
to be considered unspeakably rude to snoop around in people's
private lives without their permission. Flip over a teacup at

someone's house to see what brand of china it is, yank the label from your host's sweater to see where he got it, sniff the milk in the creamer before pouring it, and you probably wouldn't be invited back. Polite society required you to leave the cup unturned, admire the sweater from afar, pour the milk and say "thank you," even if it's past its expiration date and beginning to smell like cheese.

But lately, social norms are changing. The Internet has given rise to a culture in which our private-facing side is our public-facing side. Perpetual self-revelation is not only appropriate, it's expected. It's getting hard to tell if we're viewing someone's smooth stockinette facade, a genuinely vulnerable bumpy backside, or a new kind of reverse-stockinette-stitch fabric that's a highly edited, fictionalized version of our true selves. Each reveal is designed to give you the feeling of being intimate friends with someone who is, in fact, a complete stranger. You know how they say you can be in a crowded room and feel completely alone? Nowadays you don't even need to leave home to feel alone among the crowd.

And so we each become characters in our own movie, shoving clutter just out of the camera's view before taking that artsy picture of our breakfast. But where does our true self go? Is it really there for the whole world to see, or has it gone deeper into hiding?

I stare at the edge of that door and peer in, both curious and wary. Many parts of it please me—the camaraderie, the encouragement, the connections with all sorts of people I'd never otherwise meet. I like sharing beautiful or funny or poignant moments, offering an entertaining narrative for others and engaging in theirs.

But it's one thing to show a picture of the pretty heart someone drew in the foam of my cappuccino that morning, quite another to inform people that I'm headed to the drugstore or getting my annual gynecological exam. No, that degree of stitchery does *not* a prettier fabric make. Which is why—for now, anyway—I'll take my stockinette straight up with an old-school private side, thank you very much.

STITCH TRAFFIC

AT SOME POINT in my father's childhood, the city
planners of Battle Creek, Michigan, embarked upon
an ambitious road project designed to fix the town's
growing traffic problems. After months of planning,
the day arrived for the new changes to take effect.
With much fanfare, road crews spread throughout
the city ripping up old signs, planting new ones,
and rerouting traffic in ways that guaranteed greater
efficiency and speed. Everyone was excited.

Everyone, that is, except for the man who left
work promptly at 5 p.m., as usual, only to discover
there was no way for him to get home. The new
traffic patterns had made it technically impossible
for him to get back onto his street. Around and
around he drove until finally he gave up, parked on
a side street, and walked the rest of the way home.

This is one of my father's favorite stories. It

usually comes to mind when I'm driving and stuck in my own maze of uncooperative one-way streets. But I also think about it when I start a new stitch pattern. They're mostly pretty straightforward. A sea of stockinette. Easy ribbing, the straight and endless roads that cross the Australian Outback.

But some patterns do wild things. When you move those stacked stitches around, split them up and swap them over and under one another, force sudden merges and yields, driving becomes much more interesting. Your roads sprout new lanes, fork off in different directions, pass through busy rotaries. They can be detoured by giant bobble boulders, blasted with yarn-over potholes, or forced into sudden dead ends.

Some of the most beautiful and intricate knitted city planning comes in the form of cables and traveling stitches. They produce smooth streets that slither back and forth, soaring and diving across the fabric surface. Cables are created by intentionally reversing the chronological order of stitches, like skipping ahead in a novel. Instead of working what's next on the needles, you put those stitches aside and work the ones that follow—only then coming back to complete the stitches you left behind.

Cables are the knitter's version of highway overpasses and tunnels guiding lanes of stitches on their merry way. Usually they're worked in even pairs—one over one, two over two—for symmetry, but you can work as many or as few stitches in a cable as your imagination permits. The more stitches you overlap, the bigger the cable will be, the higher its overpass will need to be, and the deeper its tunnels must dive. Wide cables are like L.A. freeways, their beautiful maze of overpasses and off-ramps leading every stitch home. Occasionally traffic will snarl from a jackknifed big-rig, a mis-twisted cable. You'll send in a wrecker to unravel the whole thing—or maybe use the Jaws of Life to cut an outside strand and reknit your way back in.

Some patterns shake things up, veering from symmetry with a lopsided cable. Swapping many stitches over just a few produces the knitted equivalent of a tall person and a short person sharing the same umbrella. While the tall guy can never stand up straight, the short person still gets wet.

We usually nest our cables within a bed of purl stitches. This helps them "pop" visually, but it serves a deeper structural purpose, too. When you do anything out of order, it can be a source of stress. Say you have a line of people waiting to get into a movie theater, and three guys in back suddenly cut right in front of you. Folks are going to complain, right?

The same thing happens when you pull stitches out of line and jam them ahead of the ones that were patiently waiting to be knit. Knitting is an innately linear activity. Stitches love to stand in line and wait their turn. Cables disrupt this natural order. They put physical stress on the neighboring stitches, pulling some painfully tight while making others pucker awkwardly. The surrounding fabric will do whatever it can to bring the tension back to normal, and bands of purl stitches act as bumpers to absorb that jarring change in tension. We usually space our tense cable twists between smooth straightaways to let the stitches loosen their grip on the wheel and relax a little before the next bend comes.

An ambitious product marketer may insist that "true" knitters turn their cables with a cable needle, just as the guy at Williams-Sonoma will suggest that a food processor is the only real tool for chopping vegetables. A traditional cable needle is a rather stout, curved or straight object with pointed ends and a slightly thinner center. This shape allows for easy maneuvering of stitches without risk of them sliding out.

It's a pretty and helpful tool, but so is a bent paper clip, a toothpick, a coffee stirrer, a spare pen or pencil—even a bobby pin works in a pinch. You just need something to keep the first half of your hopscotching stitches safe and sound while you work on the other ones—especially if you happen to be working with a slinky silk or bamboo yarn. But some yarns, those with a lively halo of robust, high-crimp fibers, don't need a cable needle at all. The fiber ends instinctively reach out and grab the fibers around them. Those stitches will just sit there patiently waiting for you to pluck them back up and slide them onto your needle. If you're at the International Space Station for a six-month stint without your cable needle and suddenly have the urge to turn a few, rest assured, you can.

Our knitted roadways also rely on something called a "traveling stitch" to funnel traffic from lane to lane. Unlike overlapping cables, traveling stitches have no overpasses or tunnels. Their motion is derived entirely from the side-to-side movement of a stockinette road that's bordered on either side by reverse-stockinette bumps.

Traveling stitches declare eminent domain on all that they encounter, just like my Great-Aunt Kay did every time she got behind the wheel. Need to veer right? No problem, simply take whatever's there and merge it into your stockinette road. Want to pick up your great-nephew at the library? Drive your stitch onto the sidewalk and right up to the front steps. Merge successful, mission accomplished. As an added bonus, the honking of the other cars will let him know you're coming.

We merge through decreases, whether by knitting together the main road and its purl neighbor or slipping the main road, purling the neighbor, and then slipping the main road right over it. To make up for the stitch they took over when merging, they'll leave a new stitch in their wake. Traveling stitches are the driver who assumes the yield sign applies to everyone else, the nightmare freeway that is constantly merging busy lanes with no advanced notice, the great-aunt who weaves blithely from lane to curb and back again, never heeding the blaring horns of those around her. The traveling-stitch highway is a perpetual collision of lanes and cars, with the biggest one— that blundering tractor-trailer of a knit stitch—always winning.

We have many guides to choose from in the world of stitch travel, but Barbara Walker is our Rand McNally. Armchair travelers leaf through her pages and dream of the open road, mapping out stitch by stitch, turn by turn. Intrepid knitters do it when mapping out their very own journeys. And designers— the GPSs of the knitting world—do it when formulating that pattern for a hat, sweater, or scarf.

I have a friend who lives at the end of a narrow one-lane road in rural Virginia. She frequently has eighteen-wheelers show up in her front yard, their GPS having insisted that the road did something it hasn't done in nearly thirty years. One guy in Texas named his GPS Christine—for the evil Plymouth in Stephen King's horror story—after it instructed him to turn directly into oncoming traffic.

Putting blind faith in anything is rarely a good idea, whether it's a GPS or a knitting pattern. It's far better to develop your own instinct, learn for yourself what works and what doesn't—and learn *why*. Here I'm reminded of the cars my grandparents used to let my brothers and I drive when we'd visit them in Maine. First we had a VW 1500 Squareback, which my grandparents had imported from Germany in 1962. The bottom had rusted out (you could see the road through a crack on the floor) and the heat was always on. The windshield wipers moved at the speed of the engine, forcing us to keep it revved up high in the rain—until one fateful evening when the driver's side wiper gave up, bounced off the hood, and landed somewhere along the side of the road.

As challenging as the car was to drive, the Maine roads were even more so. At one spot on the winding two-lane road near my grandparents' summer house, the road curved just before a small bridge. The sign said 45 mph, but we'd never gotten close. The tires would squeal at 35 mph; our hands would cling to the dashboard for support. Somehow this idea of not being able to reach the speed limit amused us to no end.

The next year, my grandfather replaced the 1500 with a VW Rabbit he'd got cheap after an engine fire. The gas gauge didn't work, someone had scraped FUCK YOU into the paint on the roof, which had then rusted in place, and the speedometer jumped from 25 to 60 with the spastic regularity of an EKG reading. We didn't ask how it passed inspection, we were just thrilled to have a car with a radio and seat belts. Our prospects for The Curve had improved.

But by July the starter was on the fritz, forcing us to push-start the car. There were four of us and only two doors, making each ride an adventure. With my oldest brother, Jeff, steering from the open driver's door, we started to push. "OK, Clara, get in!" he'd yell, and I'd climb into the back. "Eric, go!" In went my brother, taking the spot beside me. "Janet!" His then-girlfriend hopped in the passenger seat and slammed her door shut, all three of us briefly in a moving car with nobody behind the wheel. Then Jeff slid into the driver's seat, slammed his door shut, and popped the car into gear. We held our breath, and when the engine finally lurched and sputtered to life, we all shared the smug satisfaction of having done something rather clever, like when you replace the flap in a toilet tank or turn a heel for the first time.

Later that summer the car—which by then we'd dubbed "the Shit"—lost its muffler. We began leaving the keys in the ignition whenever we parked it, but nobody took the hint. Not that they could, since it wouldn't start.

We never did make the curve at 45, not in that car or any one since. The road wants you to drive at a certain speed, and thankfully no amount of foolishness will change that. Maybe my grandparents put us in that car on purpose, knowing that its ridiculous limitations would keep our impatient recklessness in check—just as I'd never start a new knitter with laceweight yarn and slick needles. They need to do laps with a bulkier yarn first.

Then, and only then, can they develop an instinct for stitches—take curves, try new roads, give an occasional push-start, even let them get lost so we can help them find their way. Time behind the needles is the very best teacher.

Stitches are a responsibility, they are our babies. Their fate rests entirely in our hands. Each stitch needs to be considered carefully, its origin and final destination taken into account. We are the architects of their future, and they're trusting us to do right by them.

At the end of the day, we want all our stitches home safe and sound. We want to prevent anyone from taking a curve they cannot handle, or blithely driving off a cliff, confident there was going to be a bridge. And we *really* don't want the streets of our fabric to be haunted by that lost and lonely stitch who, after a long day at work, can't find his way home.

OUTED

I SPENT MY college years at a small women's liberal arts college in Oakland, California. I hadn't chosen Mills so that I could be at the forefront of the women's movement. I wasn't particularly interested in feminist studies, and I certainly didn't have an aspiration to live in a gender-divided society. No, I'd chosen Mills because my mother's best friend had graduated from there and, oh, because it had a pretty campus.

Picture an oasis of early twentieth-century California architecture: tiled rooftops, arched entryways, heavy casement windows opening to a forest of tall, fragrant eucalyptus trees, all magically hidden from the traffic and exhaust and stray gunfire of Oakland. It was a beautiful place to be, quiet and small, and safe enough for me to let down my guard and explore who I really was.

Halfway through my senior year, I finally had the courage to come out. As a knitter.

Please believe me when I say this was not a popular stance. The previous year, the college board of trustees had announced it would make Mills coed—prompting the students to strike, occupy the administrative offices, and effectively shut down the college for two weeks. Eventually, trustee Warren Hellman held a press conference and unfurled a banner: "Mills, for women, again." This replaced the earlier banner, which read, "Warren Go-to-Hell-man," which he kept until he died.

We were there to break free from the patriarchy, to experience the possibility of a world in which traditional gender roles played no part. We were unleashing our inner CEOs, Tony Award–winning playwrights, confident scientists seeking a cure for AIDS. We marched on campus, we held vigils, we studied angry books by powerful women. We learned to speak up, to question. While we weren't openly discouraged from following the path of our foremothers, the message was there.

In the midst of this amazing environment, I held on to a deep dark secret. Rolled up in a clear plastic bag under my bed was a sweater. Robin's-egg blue, with dolman sleeves, made from an exquisitely crunchy, lanolin-rich yarn from Sweden. The secret was that this sweater was only half finished, and I was the one knitting it.

When the going got rough, which it did quite a lot during college, I locked my door, curled up on my bed, pulled out the sweater and knit a few rows. If anybody knocked, I quickly shoved the sweater under the covers so they couldn't see it. Let them think it was booze or a bong or whatever typical college students were hiding.

They say that the best way to entice a person out of the closet is to show them someone like them who is living a healthy, happy, open life without fear or shame. That's what happened to me.

One day my friend Emily Jane, two years my junior and three doors down from me in the dorm, showed up with a sock in her hand. A knitted sock, on four DPNs, whose heel she was in the process of turning.

She was carrying it out in the open where everyone could see. There was no self-consciousness or even self-awareness about it. She was just turning a heel.

Before I could stop myself, I blurted out, "I knit, too!" Our mutual friend Hilair chimed in, "I'm working on an embroidered pillowcase right now."

"What are you guys talking about?" asked Jenny, my oldest and dearest friend at Mills, who lived a few doors up in the opposite direction.

"Crafty stuff," Hilair smiled.

"Emily Jane is making a sock," I said, watching Jen's face closely for signs of shock or disapproval.

"Cool!" she said. "I can't knit but I do crochet. I've been making an afghan for my Nana."

Wait, what?

And so, quite suddenly and without warning, we were all out in the open, discovering—much too late—that we each shared a quiet passion for making or adorning fabric by hand.

You know what they say, out one day, marching in a parade the next. Naturally, we needed to proselytize. But how?

We all worked as receptionists for our dorm. Most of us didn't have bigger plans on Saturday nights, so we'd usually go down to the lobby and keep whoever was working company. We decided to use this time for the Saturday Night Crafters, dragging our projects out of hiding, plunking ourselves on the mustard-colored couches in the dorm living room, and proudly stitching away. I was quite the sight with my bad perm and baggy sweatpants.

"Don't mind us," we'd volunteer to passersby, "We're just over here *crafting*." We'll be churning butter by the fire later." if you'd like to stick around." We wanted people to react more than they ever actually did.

At the time, it felt liberating. We weren't mocking our passion. We wanted to grab those legacy stereotypes and thwack them with a big sign that read, "No more." After all those Take Back the Night marches, we were taking back the craft.

All too soon we graduated and the Saturday Night Crafters disbanded forever. Emily Jane still knits, and I hope Hilair still embroiders. My Jenny died tragically in a car accident in 2004, so I'll never know if she finished that afghan for her Nana or not.

I still haven't finished that blue sweater. It sits in the same plastic bag as it did in college. Time has marched on, fashions have changed, my skills have improved. I like keeping those blue stitches in suspended animation as a sort of tribute to the past, and to my friend Jenny whose own stitches were bound off far too soon.

KITCHENERING

YOU'VE HEARD ABOUT the knitter's handshake? Two hands go in for the grab-and-shake, but at the last minute, they veer to the closest sleeve or band and grab it instead, while we ask, "Did you knit this?" Our eyes immediately scan the fabric for seams and joins, cast-on edges and edgings. We can't help it, we're wired to look for imperfections. A proper seam garners respect and admiration, even envy. Hastily worked, jagged, or lumpy lines are like scars—we know it's impolite to ask how they got there, but we can't stop staring.

My history with seams hasn't been particularly good. All my jeans used to be hemmed with tape, staples, or awkward steel safety pins that were always popping open and digging into my ankles. I avoided seams in knitting for years, instead churning out miles of garter-stitch scrolls disguised as scarves. Inevitably, I grew bored and wanted to make something substantial. I started my first sweater in 1988; its pieces are all done and still waiting for me to assemble them. The first sweater I actually *finished* was a fuzzy brushed mohair affair that had so many other problems, the sloppy seams just fit right in.

Not until I fell in love with socks did I realize how serious my seam problem was. I learned to knit socks the old-fashioned way, working a top down, flap-and-gusset pattern on four double-pointed needles. I was so excited about having turned my first heel that I temporarily forgot where I was headed. Once you reach the toe, no matter how you slice it—and we've come up with a lot of ways—you end up with stitches that need to be brought together. Because the space between foot and shoe is quite cramped and in a constant state of agitation, you can't just staple the two sides together and hope nobody notices. You need something smooth and strong, and only one stitch does the trick. It's called Kitchener.

A little background: During World War I, Field Marshal Horatio Herbert Kitchener served as Britain's Secretary of State for War. He assembled the largest volunteer army the British Empire had ever seen, his stern, mustachioed face appearing on countless posters above the words, "Wants You." He teamed up with the Red Cross to rally knitters in England, Canada, and the United States. They cranked out countless handknits for the men fighting in the trenches. Legend has it Kitchener designed a sock with a new kind of seamless toe that promised to be comfortable on soldiers' feet. That seamless toe technique is what we call Kitchener stitch today.

A lot of people liked Lord Kitchener. He'd done remarkable things while serving in the Sudan. But during the Second Boer War, he used brutal scorched-earth tactics and sent 154,000 Boer and African civilians into concentration camps, which earned him many enemies. Kitchener died in 1916 when, while traveling to Russia for peace talks, his ship was sunk by a German U-boat. His life provided fodder for six books and movies, and his death prompted conspiracy theories that still linger on. A lifelong bachelor, Kitchener was also a collector of fine china and often surrounded himself with handsome, unmarried young soldiers referred to as "Kitchener's band of boys." Which is to say that Kitchener the person was as complex as Kitchener the stitch.

For years, Kitchener the stitch eluded me. It has multiple steps that involve threading yarn through each stitch twice, just so, before letting it drop off the needle forever. The instructions are usually written in a mechanical way that tells you what to do without explaining *why*. If anything distracts you along the way, if you reverse the order of your threading by mistake, if the phone rings or your bus reaches its stop, you have no framework for realizing what's wrong and fixing it. All too easily, you'll end up with a toe that looks like a half-eaten ear of corn, which is what my first few toes looked like.

I took those early failures as a sign that Kitchener was beyond my grasp. The next few years were spent trying to navigate seams by other means, like the illiterate person who learns to say, "I forgot my glasses, could you read that for me?" when presented with a menu. Since staples and tape were out of the question, I figured out how to flip my socks inside out, line up the stitches onto two needles, and marry them off, pair by pair, in what some people call a three-needle bind-off. I call it cheating. Sure, it looked reasonable from the outside. But inside the sock, my toes were unhappy about having to share their tight space with a rude, bulky seam of stitches. Every time I side-stepped Kitchener, I felt like a flop.

You can always fudge what others don't need to see. We shove stuff into closets and under the bed before company arrives, and good manners dictate that they don't go snooping. But once something leaves your hands and goes home with someone else, all the rules change. This person has free reign to scrutinize. I gave a particularly beautiful pair of cheater-toe socks to my sister-in-law, who immediately behaved as if I'd embedded a hacksaw into both toes. To this day, no amount of explaining (and confessing) will do—she's convinced that all handknitted socks are instruments of pain. Which has conveniently gotten me out of knitting her socks for Christmas, but it also makes me feel like I've let knitting down.

As soon as I began knitting for other people, especially the likes of my sister-in-law, I realized I could no longer coast on my sloppy compromises. My pride was on the line, the entire reputation of knitting was on the line, and my friends and family deserved better. I had to work on this.

Thus began my slow journey from Kitchener dreader to true believer. While it didn't happen overnight, it was propelled by one particular collision of project and circumstances.

In my mid-twenties I was pretty sure I'd never have a child

of my own, so I was determined to become a memorable auntie for everyone else's children. I just needed my friends to start breeding. Finally, one sunny February morning, my friend Jeanne announced that she was having a baby. Showtime. This was it. I would go full-out Martha Stewart and, naturally, there would be knitting involved.

At the time, Debbie Bliss was just about our sole source for the adorable, charming, and whimsical. Among her creations was a knitted all-in-one outfit that made the wearer look like a teddy bear. It buttoned up the front, with sleeves that had attached mitts and legs with integrated booties. The hood even had two little ears. Perfect. I procured bear-worthy brown wool yarn and got the project under way. I don't think I even swatched, I just cast on and started going.

As is often the case, life intrudes. The yarn turned out to be splitty, the gauge finer than I expected, my progress tediously slow. Work got busy. Then my grandfather suddenly got sick and passed away, pulling me into that weird limbo place where my mind was mostly in the past. Things like work and relationships and knitting cute onesies for fresh new babies had no appeal whatsoever.

Fortunately, Jeanne's baby knew nothing of my life and continued to grow. Soon a beautiful little cherub named Nadiya was born. Gradually my own appetite for life returned, and I resumed work on the little brown outfit.

Debbie Bliss tends to write her patterns row-by-row, while my mind thrives in the narrative big-picture realm. This project had many odd-shaped pieces and few schematics to show me (a) what they were supposed to look like and (b) how they were all going to fit together. The only way to know was to finish knitting and hope that, in all my distraction of late, I didn't lose count or miss a crucial row, like Bugs Bunny and that notorious left turn he should've taken at Albuquerque.

The baby was crawling by the time I finally finished. Proud and relieved, I wanted to feel like I'd darned the ends of everything that had passed through my life since I began the project, that I'd converted my own sadness and sense of loss into a beautiful object that a new generation could cherish.

But something was not right. No, it was more than not right, it was wrong. Undeniably, irrefutably so. When I held up the little brown suit to admire, both feet were pointing in the wrong direction. As in backward. If you had dressed the baby using those feet as your guide, it would've seamed up the back with a hood that smothered the face. I'd knitted a cruel straitjacket with bear ears.

As I pondered what Freud would make of my mistake, I considered my options. Unraveling was not one of them, nor was tossing the whole thing into the trash. There was only one choice: I'd have to operate. No shortcuts, no glue, and no sloppy three-needle bind-offs; this baby deserved to have feet done right.

Immediately that inner voice began its "you can't do it" mantra. But for some reason, I didn't listen. I grabbed a good pair of sharp-tipped embroidery scissors and aimed them at a stitch on the ankle.

Snip.

This normally innocuous sound suddenly became loud,

like the open-mouthed crunch of a tortilla chip in a church. There was no going back. I carefully extracted the strand from its row until two shivering, opposing rounds of stockinette stitches stood before me. I turned the foot around so that it was in the proper position. Using my grandmother's darning needle for good luck and the surrounding stitches as my guide, I began slowly and carefully weaving the yarn back through the opposing loops, re-creating the arch, dip, swoop, and dive that forms each stitch.

Toss a person into a pool, and he'll either sink or swim. Chances are, if he manages to swim, he's going to be so busy staying afloat he won't have time or awareness to yell, "Hey! I'm swimming!" Likewise, I didn't yell, "Hey, I'm Kitchenering!" to the world. I just quieted my mind and did what the needle wanted to do. It worked. By the time I finished stitching up the second ankle, I felt positively invincible. Like I'd been forced to take apart an entire Volkswagen Bug and put it together again, and the car actually started. I still hadn't taught myself the science behind the why of what I was doing, but that was beside the point.

The outfit was promptly wrapped and shipped to Jeanne, who offered suitably enthusiastic praise. She slipped Nadiya into it for a picture, and I suspect that was the only time she ever wore it. That's okay. Only you and I know what *really* went into that outfit, and why I have not knit another one since.

The final nail in Lord Kitchener's coffin came several years later. I was at the Interweave offices in Loveland, Colorado, putting the finishing touches on a magazine I'd been hired to edit.

(I only edited one issue, which is all I'll say about how well *that* went.) Across the room from me sat Ann Budd, formerly managing editor of *Interweave Knits* magazine, creator of several *Knitter's Handy Book of...* books, knitwear designer, and one of my personal heroes.

She was rushing to finish a sock for a photo shoot that afternoon, and I apologized for distracting her (which I was). "Oh no, I'm almost done," she said. "I just have to finish the toe."

I gave an agonized groan, knowing just how hard the last few hundred feet of Mt. Everest can be.

"Oh, toes are eeeeeasy," she said.

I groaned again, and this time her head popped, groundhog-style, over her cubicle wall.

A minute later she was by my side, needles and yarn in hand, showing me how Kitchener was done—on a real sock that was just hours away from being immortalized on the glossy pages of a book. More than that, she explained the *why* of Kitchener. She showed me how all that convoluted threading nonsense boils down to a simple concept. You thread each stitch first in the opposite direction of how you'd go into it, and then you come back and thread it in the same direction as you'd go into it—at which point it's safe to drop off the needle. Once you get that idea, the rest falls into place.

Just imagine Mario Andretti showing you how to downshift on a curve, or Julia Child in your kitchen demonstrating the proper technique for flipping an omelet. When a hero teaches you how to do something you've struggled with for a long time, and you really *get* it, you feel fantastic.

Ever since, I've embraced every opportunity to use Kitchener for toes or anything else that requires the same level of seamless connectivity. Every time I work it, I feel clever and strong. Kitchener serves as my gentle reminder not to give up on things quite so easily. I used up far more energy finding ways to avoid this stitch than I did finally facing it head-on. Kitchener has shown me that when life unravels you, when things don't work out quite right, there's usually a good stitch waiting to put you back together again.

BRIOCHE

I LOVE TO BAKE. Depending on the day, I might even love it more than knitting. Feeding and clothing people go hand in hand, two primal human needs that were once the purview of families and communities. Today, faraway factories and machines spit out thousands of loaves of bread and up to a million articles of clothing in a single week. Those of us who still choose to make these things by hand? We've been relegated to the "artisanal" domain, creating now from choice rather than need.

Maybe it's the dough that attracts me to baking, as yarn attracts me to knitting. We manipulate both raw materials—we wrap, twist, pull, tug, tap, fold, and stir—to form something greater than the sum of its parts. Considering how symbolically similar yarn and dough are, I find it surprising that only one knitted stitch has been named after a baked good: the brioche.

Brioche is a sweet, buttery, yeasted dough that's tinted gold from eggs. It is perhaps the single most tempting dough to eat raw, its complex sweet and savory flavors balanced by a satisfying caramel-like chew. Yet when baked, it puffs up, up, up into an airy crumb of a pastry.

The traditional brioche is baked in a small round pan, slightly deeper and more angled than that of a cupcake. It emerges golden brown with its center puffed up like a giant nipple. But the dough also makes a bread that, when sliced, dredged in egg, fried crisp, and then slathered in maple syrup, has been known to make even the most discerning adults moan with pleasure.

Brioche *stitch,* on the other hand, is based on a trio of increases, slipped stitches, and decreases. Combined and repeated at regular intervals, they form both the yeast and the kneading action for your fibery dough. The resulting fabric is dense yet springy, with deep furrows that have a look of ribbed corrugation. No nipples to be found.

I think everything should be named after a baked good. People were always calling me Éclair when I was growing up. I know a parakeet in Oakland named Baguette. And if I had a child, no matter if it were a boy or a girl, I'd be sorely tempted to name it Croissant.

The croissant is the perfect knitted pastry. It is a product of slow, steady patience—and yet undeniable simplicity—involving nothing more than flour, yeast, sugar, salt, butter, and milk. These ingredients are the culinary equivalent of hearty wool fibers, perfectly willing to be all sorts of things.

As in knitting, the magic of croissants lies in the process, in what your hands *do* with the dough. After an initial mixing, kneading, and resting—the casting-on of your materials—you add the magic amalgamating ingredient: butter.

Then, it's simply a matter of rolling, folding, and chilling. You roll, fold, and chill again. The chilling and resting are perhaps the most essential parts of the process. Dough needs time to rest. Let those buttery stitches settle into their new fabric, perhaps stockinette?

A few years ago, Clare and I were stuck at home for Christmas, just the two of us in our farmhouse on the hill, while everybody else lounged by the pool with my mother in Arizona. I decided I needed a capital-P Project, something big that would keep me from feeling lonely. I looked through Julia Child's *Mastering the Art of French Cooking* to find the longest, most involved recipe—and the answer was croissants.

Her masterful recipe documents the process better than any other I've seen since. It's written clearly, helpfully, and without a hint of intimidation. I followed it, step by step, and on the third day we feasted on the most flaky, succulent, and flavorful croissants I've ever had—up there with the ones I consumed fresh daily when I lived in France. So astonished and smitten was I that I forgot to feel gloomy about being away from family over the holidays. If anything, we were both happy not to have to share our bounty with anyone else.

If the croissant is your ideal stockinette, the mille-feuille—with its "thousand" alternating layers of flaky pastry and rich cream filling—would have to be stockinette into which you've added alternating rows of frothy high-calorie cashmere, or perhaps a brushed mohair that wafts from a silky core.

Cupcakes and muffins would be the honest bobble, puffing proudly and invitingly from the fabric surface. Feather and fan is the freshly baked cannoli, its slender middle tube forming a tunnel through which the sweet mascarpone filling passes before billowing out from each end.

Garter stitch, rest its soul, would be the oft-misunderstood whole-grain bread. It's packed with body and bounce, with robust nutrition and substance. Yet it often plays second fiddle to its nemesis, the baguette. How she taunts with her perpetually skinny, perfectly tanned form. The baguette is the homecoming queen, the head of the cheerleading squad, and if you were to knit her, she'd have to be the slender, perky I-cord.

The madeleine, *my* madeleine anyway, is knitting itself. When Proust dipped one of these simple bite-sized, shell-shaped cakes in tea, the taste triggered a flood of childhood memories. It's called "involuntary memory" when a seemingly unrelated sensory experience triggers a memory. For me, a mere glance at yarn and needles—whether in our hands or someone else's—can unleash powerful recollections.

Sometimes when I'm knitting, I catch a glimpse of my reflection in a window. The mirror image of my hands alters them just enough so that they don't appear to be mine. Clear as day, they are my grandma's hands. Just one brief look, and I'm transported to a whole other dimension between past and present, a never-never land of in between.

I'm watching my grandma expertly maneuver her needle

tips and yarn in graceful, elegant arcs. I'm so young that I may not even know how to verbalize what I'm seeing, but the impression is right there, infused into my cells.

From there, I fast-forward. I'm sitting in the backseat of the car, my grandma by my side. Her hands are folded over her small brown leather purse. They're beautiful hands, small and shapely, and they do not stand still. They are in a constant state of motion, thumbs quickly orbiting one another, fingertips fidgeting, then both sets of fingers rubbing the bag's frayed leather handles. She'd stopped knitting, her mind having forgotten how—but her hands couldn't stop moving.

As time passed, she began to narrate everything she saw around her in a whispered mumble. We strained to listen, curious what her world looked like. Usually she was simply trying to remind herself what everything was. "That's the youngest boy, standing by the window…"

The narration grew more random, "Get the … yes, yes … that goes there … Good, good …" until we could not see her world at all.

My brothers and I decided that she must have engaged in top-secret government plots when we weren't around. "We bomb the embassy at midnight," she'd mumble into a secret microphone in her collar before changing quickly back to jibber-jabber when we returned to the room.

Other people have knitting memory recalls, too. "I haven't seen someone do that in ages," a stranger will smile, eyes already getting that faraway look. "My mother used to …" or "My grandmother always made us…" or "I used to do that." I'm especially fond of the men who tell me *their* knitting stories, relieved to have found a confidante who understands.

I have another memory, too: that of being a child lured by those guilty-pleasure, plastic-wrapped confections at the convenience store, products that purists might not even deign to call "pastries." I'm talking about the Little Debbie, the Ding Dong, or the ever-perky Hostess Sno Ball filled with cream, coated in marshmallow, and then rolled in bright pink coconut flakes. All were off-limits. We gazed at them longingly, assuming they tasted far better than they actually do (which I didn't discover until recently).

These blasphemous "baked" goods are the edible versions of those easy, bulky knits that deliver swift instant gratification, the sugar-high of the bind-off, while lacking any enduring nutritional value. I doubt Elizabeth Zimmermann would have admitted to knitting a "Fun Fur" scarf... but then again, who knows what pleasures she snuck secretly when nobody else was looking?

CASTING ON

BEGINNINGS ARE BEAUTIFUL things. They're the tank full of gas and the open road, a brand new notebook and a freshly filled pen. Reality hasn't had time to intrude. All you see is the vast and exciting opportunity that lies ahead.

In my knitting, I'm a starter. I go great guns at the beginning, sprinting several laps before suddenly losing my steam. It's the ongoing maintenance that I struggle with, like weeding the garden and keeping my desk clean.

Ours is a rather quiet start. While the painter stares at his blank canvas and the baker at a freshly wiped marble slab, a knitter's beginning involves an empty pair of needles and a strand of yarn. Our mission is to transform that inanimate strand of material into a luxurious three-dimensional object.

The first note in knitting—at least the simplest,

most common kind—is made with just our fingers as we wrap, pull, and tug the yarn into a slipknot. That first slipknot is the yeast of our knitted fabric, the mother stitch from which all future stitches are born. Without it, our yarn remains mute and inanimate.

Not all fabric works like this. Woven material has the benefit of two parts, the warp and the weft. Each runs perpendicular to the other. The entire length of warp is measured and tied to the loom long before the weft ever snakes its way in. Their eventual intersection locks the fabric into place, creating a firm, fluid, durable material.

But knitting is a purely monofilament creation. Like the carved stone inscriptions in Ancient Greece, knitting is "written" boustrophedonically—that is, a single strand of fiber wanders from left to right, then right to left, and back and forth it goes, building upon each row to form fabric.

We have a few rhymes for teaching children how to knit. "In through the front door," begins one, "once around the back, out through the window, and off jumps Jack." One version has Jack peeking in the window instead of jumping through it, but essentially it's the same—a sort of serial breaking and entering. We make stitches by inserting a needle into an existing loop, forming and pulling a new loop through the old one, and then dropping the old loop off the needle. That's it. Repeat for each stitch along each row, and you're knitting.

It's a bricklayer's fabric, formed by the patient and orderly placement of stitch after stitch, row by row, until—surprise— you step back and see that you've made a wall. Keep going, and you'll eventually have a strong, well-fitting home. It's no coincidence that the Three Little Pigs abandoned their wood and straw houses for a brick one. With a little thought and planning, you can arrange those same blocks into sweeping arches and open windows, jutting peaks and pointy turrets. You can add doorways and balconies and buttresses.

But it all begins with the single brick. And that first brick? More often than not, it's a slipknot.

Being the innately clever people we are, knitters have come up with endless variants to the basic cast-on. Some are firm, others stretchy. Some appear quiet, subdued. Others flaunt feathered boas or sparkly tiaras. Each has its own place.

One of the simplest and most versatile ways to create stitches is called the long-tail cast-on. Its slipknot is formed in the middle of a very long strand—hence the "tail"—of yarn. We put the slipknot-clad needle in our right hand and expertly wind the two yarn ends among the fingers of our left hand like a sophisticated game of cat's cradle. Then we make the right-hand needle swoop and dive from end to end in a graceful ballet that produces a tidy row of stretchy stitches on the needle. It's mesmerizing to watch someone really good cast on a long row of stitches this way.

Others bypass the cat's cradle machinations and simply form a series of backward loops on the needle. Beware. The backward-loop cast-on is the spare tire of cast-ons, a handy emergency patch that'll bridge short gaps and get you to the nearest gas station. It's great for small spaces like buttonholes or the thumb of a mitten, but it has no real stability or structure for larger projects. Rely on that little donut tire for a full-length road trip, and you're just asking for trouble.

If you want to put both needles to work immediately, try what's called a knitted cast-on. As Bill Murray's character in the film *Groundhog Day* was forced to repeat the same day over and over again, the knitted cast-on creates stitch after identical stitch that is never allowed to graduate from the left-hand needle to the right one. I envision the knitter saying, "Oh look, needles, I think I'll cast on!" over and over again, never remembering that she just did.

Then there's my favorite, the Charlie Brown variant called the cable cast-on. This is what my grandma taught me. It begins like a *Groundhog Day* cast-on, but instead of inserting your empty needle knitwise into that last stitch on the left needle, you slip your needle between the last *two* stitches on the left needle, as if they were a giant goalpost and your needle a trusting Charlie Brown going in for the kick. You wrap the yarn around the needle, pull the loop through, and then, at the last minute, Lucy yanks the ball and you're forced to abort the whole operation and put the new stitch back on your left-hand needle. As frustrating as the cable cast-on may be for those hopeful stitches, it's an excellent all-around cast-on that produces a nicely corded edge.

Want more flexibility? Consider the Estonian cast-on, which borrows from the long-tail cast-on but alternates the yarn positioning on your thumb and direction of your needle's swoops and dives. There's a Channel Island cast-on if you want a pretty picot-style edging like the crenellated peaks of a castle.

The German twisted cast-on will give you more stretch, ideal for a sock cuff or a collar on a top-down sweater. Need even more stretch? The tubular cast-on is for you.

Most cast-ons produce some kind of edge. But for those times when you need your stitches to look as if they appeared from nowhere, like in the toe of a sock, consider the provisional cast-on. It relies on "waste yarn" (there's an oxymoron) to create stitches you then unravel like when you unravel the stitches that seal a bag of charcoal or rice.

An equally invisible cousin of the provisional cast-on is the Turkish cast-on, which is as distinct and endearing as Turkish Delight candy is sweet and chewy. You can also play with one of the other variants popularized by Judy Becker or Jeny Staiman. Want to make a pretty, multicolored edge to, say, a colorful mitten or hat? Try the braided cast-on. Cat Bordhi popularized a moebius cast-on that creates a very Zen edge. You magically find yourself in the middle of a piece of fabric with no beginning or end. Were a tree to fall on top of it in the forest, I don't know if anyone would hear.

For all its technical nuance, I love the pure symbolism of the cast-on. It's like patting the pregnant belly of a friend, or bashing that champagne bottle on a ship's new hull. A few years ago, I began a tradition at my Knitter's Review Retreat. On Sunday morning, we all gather to embark upon a totally new project that has to be different, challenging in some way—and expressly for us. We call it our "New Beginnings" project.

When I raise my imaginary baton and give the sign, we all cast on that first row together. People are encouraged to take their knitting around the room to get good-luck stitches from one another. It's a sort of smile, a blessing, a way to capture the kinship of the event and carry it back out into the world.

I love knowing that all these happy stitches are circling the globe, scattering it with the quiet essence of knitterly goodwill. A while ago I ran into the designer Ann Budd at a conference in California. I hadn't seen her since she'd taught at my retreat that fall, and she was wearing a beautiful green sweater. I complemented her on it, and she promptly pulled out the bottom and ran her finger along the cast-on edge.

"You *should* like it," she smiled. "Your stitch is right here."

LA BELLE FRANCE

WHEN I WAS fifteen, I boarded a chartered jet at JFK
along with several dozen other doe-eyed teenagers.
We were part of the Nacel foreign exchange program
and bound for Lyon, France. I knew nothing about
where I'd be spending the next six weeks. As I waited
for my pale blue Samsonite suitcase to emerge
on the luggage carousel, I heard a funny-sounding
announcement over the PA system. "Cla-haa pahkiss?" it said. "Cla-haa pahkiss?" Which turned out
to be my name, in French.

My bag was the last one out, and they were
paging me. I sprinted to catch up with the group as
they boarded a tall, skinny bus. We drove through
the country and into a town with narrow streets and
little cars. We dragged our suitcases through a
busy square, pausing to laugh smugly at the glossy
food pictures in front of a pizza restaurant.

"Look at that!" we snorted. "You call that a pizza?"

"Not like in Baltimore," said one kid. "We've got the best pizza."

"No way, man," interrupted another, "I'm from Chicago. You can't get better pizza than ours." We all gasped at the last picture: Someone had cracked an egg on the pizza. A whole egg. Gross.

We finally reached a train station and said our good-byes as the group split into smaller clusters. Five of us were put on a train with a kind but rather tired-looking woman. As the train began to move, she focused her clipboard on me. "Cla-haa," she began. "Ear ees zee ann-formacion abouuut zee fai-milie whair you wheel be stayeeeng." It turns out I was headed to Nîmes, where Jacques, his wife, Marianne, and their daughter, Sophie, were waiting for me. My life in France was about to begin.

I soon learned that Jacques and Marianne were in fact not married at all. They'd fibbed to the agency so they could get an exchange student. My host sister, Sophie, was Jacques's only daughter from a previous marriage. She adored her papa, worshiped The Cure and James Dean ("zee cure" and "jomms deeeen"), and detested Marianne.

Jacques was a stereotypical Frenchman. He was short, had slightly hunched shoulders, was always puffing on a Gauloises cigarette, and maintained a contemptuous sneer for all that displeased him. He was estranged from his father, a famous actor I would see years later on the stage in Paris. He studied ancient mythology and was an abstract artist. He openly wept during a tribute to the late Jacques Brel, which he made me watch with him on the TV.

Marianne belonged to that generation of women whose personality was formed primarily by those around her. She was warm and friendly, recently divorced, and had two grown children of her own. She had dyed brown hair, a propensity for large, shapeless dresses, and an overdeveloped maternal instinct that made her speak to me like I was an eight-year-old—fitting, since my French language skills were at about that level.

Sophie was petulant, competitive, occasionally hyper, and inclined to baby talk when in the company of her father.

Our home was the top three floors of a tiny stone building in the center of Nîmes. Centuries of footsteps had worn down the stone stairs until they had a deep U in the center, giving the stairwell the feel of a Mediterranean luge run. The thick walls kept out some of France's *midi* heat, but at midday we still had to close all the metal shutters to keep the sun out. Each evening, strains of the theme song from *Dallas* drifted over the tiled rooftops, mixed with the high-pitched squeaks of birds and occasional stray notes from the piano bar at the end of the street. Fifteen minutes to closing time, the pianist would always play Elton John's "Sorry Seems to Be the Hardest Word."

Every few days we'd pack into Jacques's bright orange vintage Datsun coupe and speed through the countryside, Sophie and I squeezed in back on either side of their large, panting spaniel, Duduche. Up front, a cloud of cigarette smoke; in back, hot, wet dog breath.

We went to the ocean, where I had my first taste of passion fruit in the smallest scoop of ice cream I'd ever seen. We climbed to the top of a Roman aqueduct, we swam in cool, slow-moving rivers. We visited a shopping mall—very new and exciting in those days—and passed a yarn store full of pastel-colored skeins, all identical in shape and all frighteningly fine in gauge. We sped along ancient tree-lined routes to Avignon and Valence and to a tiny town called Beauchastel, where Marianne and her children had a summer home. There we met Marianne's son, Christophe, a bronzed, blue-eyed god recently returned from a spiritual pilgrimage to India. Sophie's mood improved immediately.

We prepared feasts at the summer house and sat out under shady trees at a rickety table with mismatched chairs. I watched mayonnaise being made by hand. One day I was in the kitchen with Marianne's daughter, Mylène. She was knitting a light-blue baby sweater out of a fine-gauge wool just like the kind I'd spotted days before. I was thirsty, so I asked her for a . . . a . . . um . . . She put down her knitting, held up a glass, looked me straight in the eye, and said *"verre."* I can't say why, exactly, but that moment marked a turning point in my French language immersion.

I'd arrived having studied French for only two years, the first of which barely counted because it was with a permanent substitute who didn't speak the language herself. I went to the same school as my older brother, and he'd fared so badly in French that when I arrived and Madame Gehrels had to shuffle overflow students to the sub, she saw my last name and must have muttered an emphatic *"non!"*

So I'd arrived in France with a basic *Le Petit Prince* under-standing of verbs and nouns, but I could barely function fluidly in any kind of everyday setting. This trip was my baptism by fire. No computer, no Google translator, no Internet even. Nobody in the house really spoke English, and I certainly couldn't call home, long-distance rates still being a splurge.

And so, by some combination of survival instinct and skill, I managed to stay afloat and eventually to swim. That day in the kitchen when Mylène held up the glass I was trying to ask for and said "*verre,*" something in my mind clicked, or surrendered, or did whatever minds do when they stop fighting. I let go and began thinking in French. Soon Sophie and I were memorizing lyrics to popular songs and singing them together. We made up silly new verses, we whispered secrets to one another, I began to dream in French, and I even started cracking jokes that made people laugh.

My mother had lived in Paris in the early 1960s on a Fulbright scholarship, and I'd grown up gazing longingly at her black-and-white pictures. This was nothing like those pictures, but it was still magical. I loved how different everything was—how thin the writing paper was, how funny my desk lamp looked, how smooth the light switches were. I got hooked on writing with a fountain pen, drinking from tiny glasses, and tearing off pieces of bread to wipe my plate clean. I became an expert at bathing in a tub instead of a shower.

Until then, my only reference for picnics was thick peanut butter sandwiches and a warm plastic canteen of tap water, followed by a bruised banana. But here we perched on a hillside in Provence and ate buttery cheeses on fresh baguettes, followed up with big chunks of chocolate, all washed down with bottled water infused with sugary fruit syrups (no wine for me).

I took the family to see a performance of Puccini's *Turandot*, which was staged outdoors in a Roman amphitheater. We rode a creaky little Ferris wheel and watched fireworks for July 14, Bastille Day. I was even tempted to go back to that yarn store and pick up some fine-gauge wool of my own. I loved everything—the cadence of the culture, the sounds of the words coming out of my mouth. I never wanted to speak English again.

All too soon it was time to leave. On my last night there, over ice cream parfaits at the piano bar at the end of the street, we tearfully promised to keep in touch—and in my heart, I vowed to return.

Back home in Tucson, I became that insufferable snob who started all her sentences with, "Well, in France..." I used to lie in bed with my Walkman, eyes closed, listening intently to the tape recordings I'd made of my street—its cars, birds, music, footsteps. What a jolt to open my eyes and find myself so far away.

As soon as the ink dried on my high school diploma, I was back in France for the summer, sipping a grand-crème at the Cafe Flore in Paris before boarding the TGV for Valence, where Marianne would meet me and take me back to her summer home. But it was different. Sophie was more sullen, Marianne seemed needy, and Jacques wasn't there. At first they said he was too busy with work to join us, but then Marianne confided in me that they were having problems. My language skills had improved to the point where she didn't need to talk to me like an eight-year-old, and what she did say made it clear I'd stepped into a difficult situation. I was relieved to take the train back to Paris for the rest of the summer.

Again, in college, France pulled me back. I spent my junior year in Paris studying at the Sorbonne. It wasn't just the fountain pens and the funny light switches that kept drawing me back. I'd discovered a sort of parallel universe in France, and I liked it infinitely better than the one back home. They say that people acquire the traits of the dominant culture associated with the language they speak—they almost have a different personality with each language. I certainly did, and my alternate Clara was a charming antidote to all that troubled me. It was like a comforting cloak of invisibility.

Gradually, a problem revealed itself: The closer I got to fluency within French culture, the more I was identified as American. If France's cultural fabric were made from that superfine baby-blue wool Mylène had been knitting, I—no matter how hard I tried—was a big, goofy brushed mohair. If I tamed my halo, twisted myself tight, tucked in my ends, I could almost pass from afar—people thought I was Swiss, or Danish, the cultural equivalent of mohair passing for a shimmery Wensleydale—but the minute I opened my mouth, my true nature revealed itself. Not because of how I spoke, but rather because of the underlying structure of how I thought, saw the world, reflected, and responded. I could change my twist and ply, but I couldn't do anything about my cellular makeup.

I finished college and returned yet again, this time through a fellowship with the French government. I was an *assistante*, a sort of tutor-slash-babysitter for high school English students.

I was placed in the northwest city of Nantes, the birthplace of Jules Verne and the hub of the French slave trade. Whereas my previous trips had allowed me to quietly assimilate into the culture, this time my whole raison d'être was to be a foreigner—which literally translates as "stranger." My dreams of disappearing behind the cloak of French culture couldn't materialize. I'd been hired to be different—to be l'Américaine.

We were given two days' training in how to teach English. My favorite lesson was the afternoon we were taught how to operate a VCR. The teacher spoke to us slowly and carefully, pointing to the button marked PLAY, explaining what it did.

School began. I was a lousy teacher. I saw the same students only twice in a month, making serious continuity impossible. When "How was your weekend?" failed, I resorted to games, having students fill in the empty speech bubbles in Calvin and Hobbes cartoons, or translate the lyrics to "Hotel California." Finally I gave up and showed everybody the ancient copy of the movie *Manhattan* I'd discovered in the media library.

The teachers were friendly enough, but they never let me forget my otherness. One morning I'd arrived in my French attire, dressed up in a little skirt with my tights, clunky leather shoes, thin wool coat, and a wool scarf I wrapped around and around my neck as I'd seen my students do in crowded hallways (thwacking me in the face as they wrapped them). I confidently clip-clopped into the teacher's room, which still had a mimeograph machine, and one of the English teachers came up to me. "Ohhh, Cla-haa," she cooed, "Have you hurt your neck?"

Meanwhile, the school concierge, a great fan of Westerns,

discovered I grew up in Arizona and would stage a mock shoot-out every time I came and went. "Ehhh, Cla-haa!" he'd yell from his tiny windowed room by the front gate. "Pow, pow, pow!" he'd shoot his imaginary guns before putting them back in his imaginary holsters. "Eye amme zee cow-buye, yaah?"

When my year was up, I no longer believed I could escape and become someone else in France. As charming as French Clara was, my cloak of invisibility was wearing thin. There was no getting away from the fact that French Clara's brain and American Clara's brain were one and the same. I knew I could stay in France until I was ninety and people would still call me l'Américaine—and that wasn't what I wanted. I'd also come to realize that brushed mohair is actually quite pretty when you give it space to bloom.

A week before I left France, I went to a used bookstore to sell some of my books. While the clerk was looking through my collection, I browsed the shelves. A familiar voice came across the aisle. "Mais non, ce n'est pas possible," it began. "C'est la petite Américaine... Cla-haa?"

I glanced up to see Jacques—my Gauloises-puffing Jacques from that first summer. He had just moved to Nantes for a teaching position at the university. We quickly caught up. Sophie lived in the south with a boyfriend. They had a baby. He and Marianne had long ago split up. He was with a new woman. I'd like her, he said. I'd have to come and have dinner with them before I left. They didn't have a phone yet, so I gave him my number and we parted. After a quick trip to Rome to visit family, I returned to find that my roommates—all of whom were also leaving—had disconnected our phone line. I left France for the last time without ever seeing Jacques again.

It's been twenty years since that visit and since I stopped trying to lose myself within someone else's fabric. I like to think my life fits my fiber far better now. I've relaxed into an open stitch pattern that highlights the mohair instead of trying to squash it. But I still long to go back to France. Whenever I'm on deadline, I'll have at least three different browser windows open, each featuring a charming rental cottage or apartment somewhere in France. The worse the deadline, the bigger the house and the longer-term the rental.

Part of me fears that the Clara I've become will still be sideswiped, if given the chance, by her long-dormant French counterpart. I worry that my beautiful life may suddenly seem once-again insufficient in the face of that alluring, smooth, tightly twisted worsted world. Or maybe France has changed, too? Maybe its fabric has relaxed to accommodate more variety. Perhaps now it would accommodate my fuzzy halo, and the two Claras could finally become one.

CHANNELING
JUNE CLEAVER

THEY SAY THAT beauty is only skin deep, that it's what's *inside* that really counts. All this is fine, well, and good, but what about pie? You could have the most exquisite filling known to mankind, but if your dough is a flop, nobody's going to want a slice.

For years, piecrusts have eluded me. One New Year's Eve, I wrote a bucket list of things I'd like to accomplish before I leave this earth. Somewhere between "write a book" and "take off a year and travel to India," I added "master piecrust."

When I was growing up, nobody ever seemed excited about crust. They never hummed as they rolled it out; there was always a sense of obligation and dread as they waited for it to tear (it always did) or stick (it always did) or otherwise spontaneously combust somewhere between the rolling pin and pie plate.

My health-conscious mother made her crusts out of whole wheat flour, experimenting with various oils and "heart smart" alternatives to butter and Crisco. The pies of my childhood were always a bit dry, crumbly, slightly bitter in taste. Their tops were made from a patchwork of torn pieces that had been glued back together. And they were always served with the unspoken message, "Eat this damned thing."

Living in Maine in a house overlooking acres of blueberry fields, blueberries figure prominently in my summer diet. I've mastered blueberry crumbles, blueberry pancakes, blueberry syrup . . . but every time someone visits—and many do—the first thing they ask for is pie.

How I've longed to be one of those June Cleaver people who can happily whip up the perfect pie at a moment's notice. What's that you say? A busload of tourists is stranded at the town hall, and they need two dozen blueberry pies for sustenance? Not a problem, let me just don my apron. Can I knit them some mittens while I'm at it?

But the ominous nature of pie dough has always taken the wind out of my sails. When you hear people groan about something enough times, it's easy to groan about it yourself—even if you've yet to give it a fair shot. People do this with knitting all the time. "Thumb gussets are impossible," they say. Only after we follow the instructions, step by step, do we realize how incredibly graceful, logical, and downright *easy* a thumb actually is.

Funny enough, I managed to write a book—three, actually—before I felt ready to turn my attention to pie dough. After multiple failures, each adding a new layer to the compost pile,

I stumbled upon the golden recipe: the 3-2-1 Pie Dough from Michael Ruhlman's *Ratio*. This combination of ingredients (flour, fat, and liquid) and technique produces the dreamiest piecrust known to man.

It goes against all common pie dough wisdom. While everybody blends some mix of butter and Crisco, this one calls for nothing but pure, unadulterated butter. And everybody warns, "Do not overwork!" Yet I roll, fold, slap, and tease this dough to within an inch of its life. The final product? Airy and crisp, rich and buttery, both ethereal and substantial. Even when disaster strikes—like the time my nephew placed a ten-pound doorstop on the center of a particularly perfect blueberry-lemon pie—it still comes out beautiful, in its own way.

Not only did Michael Ruhlman help me get over my fear of piecrusts, he also gave me a chance to overcome my fear of introducing myself to famous people. Not that I succeeded, but I certainly did try. I was in Cleveland to film yarn-related segments for the PBS television show *Knitting Daily TV*. I'd arrived at the airport with my suitcase of swatches and TV-ready jewel-toned shirts, my freshly lacquered nails shining in the light. The weeks leading up to the trip had been a frenzy of swatching, researching, and fretting.

I was waiting for the producer and crew to arrive when I noticed another man waiting in the area. Our pacings crossed, and I glanced at his face. Without a doubt, I'd just walked past Michael Ruhlman.

I am not a person who walks up to famous people and introduces herself. First of all, I almost never see famous people—

or if I have, I certainly didn't recognize them. I'm always the clueless one in the group who turns around too late and says, "Huh?" after the person has passed. Second, I don't think most famous people would much care who I was. Third, and perhaps most important, I think everybody deserves a little privacy. When fate put me in an elevator with knitting luminary Barbara Walker, I let her dictate the conversation. (She was charming, and I learned that her husband does the dishwashing in their house.)

But this wasn't just any random celebrity, it was the man who'd helped me check an item off my bucket list. He'd been in my kitchen, helping me delight and harden the arteries of countless friends and family members. He'd made me a pie person. That deserved thanks, don't you think?

After a few more minutes of pacing, my nervousness was annoying even to myself. How different was this than frogging lace or turning a cable without a cable needle? *Don't let fear stop you,* I told myself. *Walk through it. You'll regret it if you don't.*

So I did. My hands sweating, my heart in my chest, I walked up to him.

"Mr. Ruhlman?" I'd read that you're supposed to address celebrities by their last name out of respect. Unfortunately, my voice was so quiet that he didn't hear me. But the eye contact and my moving mouth made him stop. He looked down at me, taller than a redwood he was. There was no annoyance in his gaze, only the slightly concerned look one would give to, say, an escapee of an asylum.

My mouth opened and out came, "I just wanted to thank you for your pie dough recipe. It totally transformed my entire relationship to pie." Only mush those words together and say them in a very high-pitched warble. While we shook hands, I babbled something about how honored I was to share an airport with him. By now my ears were buzzing, my face an electric shade of fuchsia. I bowed a few times more before turning around and walking away as quickly as I could, narrowly missing a concrete pillar. I was mortified, yet also exhilarated to have faced a fear and wobbled my way through it.

I know some people can feel invincible after bungee jumping or diving out of an airplane (assuming they survive) or even after cutting a steek for the first time, and that's exactly how I felt. At that moment nothing seemed scary, not pie dough, not introducing myself to a hero, not talking intelligently about yarn to a much larger television audience. It all seemed quite human and achievable and, for some reason, utterly funny. When you strip us all down to our essence, removing the pedestals and the frippery, we're all just people.

"Where are you?" my phone buzzed. It was the show's executive producer. "We've landed. Heading to baggage claim."

Back to reality, but all those nerves and butterflies were gone. I tackled the show and had a blast.

When I got home, you can be sure I baked a celebratory pie—this one a glorious cherry creation with a woven lattice top. It wasn't for visiting friends or family, or for that busload of stranded tourists down at the town hall. It was just for me—and it was, on both the outside *and* the inside, perfect.

PABLO CASALS, GRANDPA, AND ME

FROM THE AGE of ten, cellist Pablo Casals began
every day with a walk. Then he'd return home and
perform two J. S. Bach preludes and fugues on the
piano. "It fills me with an awareness of the wonder of
life, with a feeling of the incredible marvel of being
a human being," he said in *Joys and Sorrows: Reflect-
ions by Pablo Casals as Told to Albert E. Kahn.* "Every
morning of my life I see nature first, then I see Bach."

My paternal grandfather cut this quote out
of a magazine and taped it to the downstairs china
closet, right above his black rotary phone, partially
obscuring the view of my grandma's blue Royal
Worcester breakfast set. It was directly across from
a tiny powder room with red, white, and blue wallpaper dating back to the bicentennial. I passed that
piece of paper for years before ever reading it, but
the words have stayed with me.

My grandpa was a disciplined man. Accomplished in his field, methodical to a fault. He ate the same lunch every day for forty years: one can of kippered herrings and two rye crackers that cost him "exactly twenty-seven cents" from the Navy commissary. (My mother refuses to acknowledge inflation when she tells the story. It was, and shall forever be, twenty-seven cents.) He wore the same few suits and ties until they were threadbare. One pair of L.L.Bean shoes kept him suitably shod for most of his retired life, just over nineteen years.

Bach was his hero, and he had little tolerance for anything else. My father once played him a Puccini aria, and he snorted, "What's *her* problem?" He didn't have much patience for my own music, either, although I did try to introduce him to The Sugarcubes, not realizing that the album cover I kept showing him featured line drawings of naked people. Oops.

My grandpa idolized Casals, a man he'd heard perform in Europe and whom he felt could genuinely interpret the mathematical beauty of Bach. I used to think my grandpa also held on to Casals's words because they validated his own need for order, for the comfort of routine.

In his work as a solar physicist, my grandpa changed our understanding of the sun's ultraviolet spectrum. He was a scientist, his mind a sort of cell-based supercomputer able to process vast amounts of data. Taking leaps and trusting the unknown, those were completely foreign to his nature. Everything new had to be studied, evaluated, its merits and pitfalls dissected, poked, and prodded to within an inch of its life. He didn't get elected to the National Academy of Sciences for waving his hands in the air and saying, "Oh hell, let's give it a go and see what happens."

As an impetuous teenager, this drove me nuts. Who *cares* which air conditioner we get? They're all going to break in a few years anyway. But my grandpa knew that if he crunched the data, he'd be able to figure out which machine really was the best. Toward that end, *Consumer Reports* magazines were always on the dining-room table. Appliance salesmen who knew him rolled their eyes when they saw him coming.

One summer was dedicated to the question of whether or not my grandparents should replace the refrigerator on the porch. It was an ancient machine with a round condenser on the top and a heavy door that clicked when it opened and closed. It never kept the ice cream quite cold enough. But was it the freezer's fault? My grandpa had discovered that the local IGA sold ice creams for half price if they'd been melted and refrozen in transit. Every night we'd pull out a rectangular box of Sealtest ice cream, always in odd flavors like rum raisin or butter almond or Neapolitan, and ladle runny scoops into our dessert bowls. The refrigerator was never replaced.

I always felt that my grandpa was trying to control everything. But now I wonder. Just as planning a meal can be more fun than actually eating it, maybe he was more enchanted with the *investigation* of things than with the outcome. If he'd been a knitter, he would have made one heck of a swatcher.

The word *swatch* dates back to the 1600s, when it referred to a sample piece of cloth attached to a batch of fabric being sent to the dye house. Today, a swatch represents a small piece of knitted fabric we create as a sample. We swatch (the verb) as practice, as a musician practices her scales, to keep our fingers nimble and improve our technique. The more you do something—whether it's a B-flat scale or purling three stitches together through their back loops—the easier it becomes.

Swatching is also the knitter's equivalent of sight reading. It's that first read-through when we meet a new piece and figure out how it should be played. Our answer comes in the form of a number, called gauge. Gauge is to knitting what scale is to the map, an utterly necessary device if you plan on traveling any particular distance. Gauge is expressed in terms of the number of stitches required to fill a certain amount of fabric when knit on a specific size of needle. It is the beginning of a recipe to help you transpose what you see into what you make, a knitterly version of the tablespoon, the measuring cup, the oven thermometer. In a world that's entirely handmade, gauge provides a welcome compass point to keep us from getting lost.

The smaller your gauge number is, the bigger each stitch will be, the fewer you'll need in order to complete your project, the less yarn you'll need, and the faster you'll reach your destination. The higher your number, the smaller each stitch is, the more stitches you'll need, the more yarn, the more time. Those tiny stitches are the Sunday drivers of knitting. Slow progress, but what a pretty ride.

Gauge also functions like a speed limit. We're given a number and told to follow it in order to enjoy the yarn at its optimal capacity. Nimble yarns can take curves at a speed that'd wipe out a bulky yarn, like a tiny speedboat can out-maneuver an oil tanker. Every yarn has its ideal range; almost every yarn lists this range on its label.

We have our cautious drivers, those who clutch the wheel with both hands and always obey the law. Their eyes dart back and forth between road and speedometer, foot jamming on the brakes or quickly accelerating to maintain the exact speed. It's not much fun to be a passenger in their car.

The footloose and fancy-free knitters, new ones especially, get so caught up in the glory of being behind the wheel, feeling the wind blowing in their stitches for the first time, that they often forget about speed completely. The lucky are protected by a wide, empty road, a large and forgiving vehicle, that guardian angel who manages to get their attention in time. Which is why many of us started with the scarf, a humble rectangle equipped with training wheels and extra airbags to keep us upright and safe until we have a few more miles behind us.

Early knitters had few yarn labels to guide them, no posted gauge or printed pattern to follow. The needles were placed in their hands at such an early age that a sort of instinct developed. It told them how to kick-start their stitches, how fast to take certain curves, when to slow down, how to swap strands after a blowout. Without having to think about it, their hands knew how to tweak their fabric until it gave the results they wanted. From this, they were able to measure and calculate, with simple hatch marks on a piece of paper, until they had the blueprints for their sweater. They didn't rely on anyone else's signposts or numbers, and the results were stunning.

Today, we depend on the instructions of others—we let

iPads guide our pilots, we work from recipes and patterns written by someone else. In the knitting world of "someone else," gauge becomes the crucial promise. It is the synchronizing of watches before an important mission, the sacred pact between leader and follower. "If you drive on this road at this exact speed," it seems to say, "you will reach Peoria at 11:37 a.m. like I did." Peoria is a sweater that actually fits.

You can tell a lot about people by how they view swatching. For the eager knitter, the gauge swatch is the mother who yells, "Come back and get your raincoat in case it rains!" when you're already halfway across the front yard. You want to get started on that glorious new sweater *now*, and the pattern is saying you have to sit inside and waste time knitting a square? Swatching is the ounce of prevention, the nightly flossing, the benchmark colonoscopy at sixty. Not very sexy, but highly recommended.

Some dutifully come back inside and knit their square. But others keep running and elope, casting on for that project without really getting to know the yarn first. Is it smooth or splitty? How much bounce does it have? Will it want coffee in the morning, or tea? "Who knows?" they say. "I'll figure it out as I go along." Far more knitters go on a few dates, ignore the signs, and marry the wrong yarn anyway, convinced they can change it. Sometimes they actually can, but usually not.

Because of my work, I am a serial swatcher, unable to commit and settle down. Every week, I meet a new yarn. I often fall in love and decide *this* is the one. I make plans to settle down. I choose my china, I wallpaper the nursery. But the clock keeps ticking, and soon a new yarn knocks on the door. I swatch it out of professional curiosity, I file my report, and soon enough I've fallen in love again. It's exhausting.

But there's a third reason to swatch. Not for practice, and not to get your gauge, but for the very reasons Pablo Casals touched upon in his quote: to transcend. There is a calm, meditative act in forming stitch upon stitch, divorced of any particular objective or deadline. In transcendental swatching, the journey takes precedence over the destination.

It's how Paul Theroux swatched when he wrote *The Old Patagonian Express*, focusing not on his time in Patagonia but on his *getting there*. When you swatch to transcend, you're taking a yarn for its morning walk, working stitches from memory alone, celebrating the faint vibration of fiber sliding against needle. You're following Pablo Casals's entire morning routine wound up into one beautiful ball of yarn.

Just over the hill from my house is a large freshwater pond that's quite possibly the best place on earth. My brothers and I learned to swim there as children, and that pond is part of what lured me back to Maine after so many years in San Francisco. In the summer, I like to swim out beyond the farthest float and then stop. My arms and legs slowly move back and forth, keeping me afloat in the soft water. With the "action" part of my mind happily occupied with its familiar task, the rest of my mind—the part that dreams and chews on conundrums— is unleashed and allowed to run. I'm not there to burn calories and get my heart rate up, I'm not racing with anyone. I'm in the water to be in the water, to tread through my thoughts, and that's all. Sometimes, if I hold perfectly still, the loons will sing.

That's what transcendental swatching is all about. Tethered by the familiar and predictable physical motions, our mind is free to float up, up, up into the sky. Whenever we drift too far, a dropped or snagged stitch will pull us back to the present. We focus and fix before flying again. To the outsider, it may look like I'm working on a humble-looking square, but my mind is making huge blankets, ambitious turtlenecks, perfect-fitting cardigans. I'm orchestrating vivid scenes, sorting out problems, traveling to faraway places, while the only finger I'm actually lifting is the one required to form each stitch.

Whenever Casals went through the physical motions of his familiar walk and Bach preludes, his mind and spirit were free to wander—and the fruits of those wanderings were the foundation of his day. My grandfather didn't knit, didn't really swim, couldn't play a cello to save his life. And he certainly didn't take walks every morning. But he did listen to Bach every day, and he did research everything he touched. I swatch every day, and I, too, tend to research everything my fingers touch. My grandfather frustrated me so as a child, but maybe I'm more like him than I ever imagined. Our lives followed decidedly different paths, but we both seem to have found similar ways to dip our toes into the cosmos.

THE DROPPED STITCH

EVERY THURSDAY morning for the last eight or so years, I've had a standing coffee date with my friend Pam. Our success rate is about fifty percent, but each week we still try. I've grown accustomed to sitting and waiting, pulling out work to entertain myself. Eventually I'm either interrupted by her familiar voice or by the realization that I've been stood up yet again.

Sometimes life intrudes, and occasionally I'm the one who doesn't show up. Other times, we go out of our way to email in advance and formally sched-ule our coffee. Really, we're going to do it this time. "Yes, I'll see you then," we say. "Nine-thirty sharp." But it doesn't happen.

It's a funny thing when you're left sitting alone at a table for two, expectantly gazing at an empty chair. Left untended, the mind easily wanders into that perilous land of past abandonments, mulling over the lowest moments in agonizing detail. Suddenly I'm no longer sitting at Coffee By Design, I'm a fourteen-year-old freshman at University High School in Tucson, Arizona. It's lunchtime, and I'm purposefully walking back and forth between the two main buildings just to avoid the painful prospect of sitting alone in the cafeteria, which I did for three solid months until I discovered the drama club.

Not that I mind eating alone now. I cherish it. I get to eat where I want, order what I want, and enjoy my own company. I can stare into space, read a book, or eavesdrop on other people's conversations to my heart's content. But it's harder when you're staring at a chair where someone was supposed to be. How easy it is to take that absence personally, to assign it far deeper meaning than it deserves. How embarrassing to say, "No, I'm expecting someone," when someone asks to borrow the chair—and then watch it sit so conspicuously empty.

With Pam, a decade of friendship has taught me that it really isn't about me, it's more about how she lives, manages her time, and moves through the world. I am just one of many stitches on her busy needle.

And then the call comes, usually thirty-four minutes later. I'm tempted not to answer, because what kind of fool waits half an hour for someone to show up? Me, that's who.

"Clara!" She always sounds jubilant, as if she's just discovered a $100 bill in her coat pocket. "Are you still there?"

Of course I am.

"It'll have to be a quickie," she always says.

"Of course," I always say. "I'll be here."

The thing is, it never is a quickie, and that's what keeps me coming back. Once she sits down and we start talking, the connection returns instantly. We take up exactly where we left off. I forget I was alone or that I doubted she would return, and I simply enjoy the happy comfort of a friend's company.

Stitches are social creatures, too. They long for connection. Only during the moment of conception do they sit alone on your needle, drumming their fingers on a table set for two. They wait for their neighbor to join them and make the fabric complete—for a stitch always needs neighbors in order to be fully realized. Alone, it can do little. Stack even one solitary stitch on top of another and you start to have something. Add a few friends on either side, more voices to the choir, and your fabric grows cohesive and beautiful. A community of sorts.

Before those friends come to claim it, a lone stitch can be somewhat unsure of itself. It has nothing to hold it in place and keep its dreams alive but the force of twist and crimp, memories of past loops, and anticipation of future needles. It doesn't always see the big picture of what it's going to become. It only knows that it's hooked into the guy below, hopefully has someone to hold its hand on one side or the other, and will eventually be secured by someone upstairs. Those are the hopes of pretty much every knitted stitch.

Should the unimaginable happen—should that loop of a stitch inadvertently slip from your needle's grasp and be set free—you will quickly learn everything you need to know about that yarn's true character.

Yarns are like people. Some have abandonment issues. They don't do well when stood up. They look at the empty chair, they check their watches and realize what's happened, and they panic. Glancing around, they see happily secure stitches just out of grasp, mocking, sneering, like teenagers in a cafeteria. They look up for the reassuring arms of the next row, but they see only air.

The first instinct of a fretful yarn is to flee the scene of embarrassment. In most fabrics, the nearest exit runs straight down through row after row of comfortably seated stitches. The fretful yarn may upturn everything in its path—chairs, tables, trays of half-eaten Tater Tots and chicken nuggets—until finally, like a dog on a leash, it's stopped in its tracks by a firm yank of the cast-on row.

But not all yarns respond in this way. Some stand their ground, not the least bit unnerved by their disconnection or solitude. Their stitches can sit suspended for hours, days, *years* even. They bring their own books. They write letters home. They nod to passersby, reach out to pet strangers' dogs, completely confident that eventually someone will notice their absence and come back to pick them up. "Oh, hello there," they finally greet the returning needle, sliding in quickly and putting on their seat belt. "Nice to see you again."

What makes a yarn react to abandonment the way it does? Why do some people crumble when faced with that empty chair, while others take it in stride? Does it all boil down to confidence—spunk, determination, security in one's self and one's own place in the world? Ironically, the most opulent and imperial yarns—the ones with slick and glossy surfaces that glide past their neighbors without so much as a how-do-you-do—tend to slink out the emergency exit the fastest.

Whether it's from vanity or perhaps shyness, these slippery silks and smooth worsteds seem to have fewer deep and abiding connections. They look so beautiful in the skein. Their smooth and dense construction may help them last longer in the world. But what kind of life do they have? They're so intent on holding it together that they rarely relax, let their hair down a little, get to know their neighbors. They sit upright in their fabric, arms held in to preserve their personal space. Knit them too loosely and sunlight will stream in between each stitch; too tight, and the stitches quickly get grumpy and stiff from the forced intimacy. They expect life to go a certain way.

As you can imagine, when crisis strikes and this stitch suddenly finds itself teetering alone on a high ledge, it rarely knows whom to call, who may be home at this hour, which neighbor might have the tallest ladder. And the neighbors? Well that's the problem, because they're usually all made from the same stuff. Unless true disaster strikes, most doors will close and the abandoned stitch will be left sprinting for that red EXIT sign.

But those yarns with outgoing personalities—the ones formed from a noisy and jubilant community of lofty, crimpy fibers that are always in one another's business—those yarns come together in times of trouble. Each stitch, even the tormented teenager who just wants a little privacy now and then, fundamentally supports the others. They willingly expand and contract to fill whatever space you give them. Need to add three more place settings for dinner? No problem, they smile, we can stretch the meal. And when the needle suddenly disappears and leaves a stitch stranded, the others reach out instinctively. "We've got your back," they say, and they mean it.

These are the good, old-fashioned woolen-spun yarns like your proverbial (and my actual) grandmother used to knit, made from shorter, jumbled fibers that are allowed—even encouraged—to protrude and mingle. I'm talking about the more traditional farmhousey yarns of yore, those fuzzy Shetlands, spunky Finns, even the occasional sumptuous Merinos. Therein lies the rub, for despite their humble appearance, these yarns can sometimes contain the most tender and luxurious of fibers. But instead of uniform smoothness, these have bounce and body, smiling eyes, a ready laugh.

Depending on where you go, these rugged-seeming woolen-spun yarns may not be sitting at the popular kids' table. In fact, they're more likely to be sitting in smaller groups outside, on the grass, under a quiet tree. But you know what? When push comes to shove comes to slipped needle and dangling stitch, when a chair is empty that's supposed to have someone sitting in it, those are the yarns that will always wait for you. They are loyal to a fault, forgiving and secure in their own twist and tenacity. You want them on your side.

BEATING THE BIAS

IN MY LIFETIME of knitting, I can count on one hand the number of projects I've knit out of pure cotton. Ditto linen and hemp. I admit with regret and resigned determination that I have a personal bias toward protein fibers—things grown on the backs of animals—that leaves me predisposed to avoid fibers grown on seed and stalk. Like cotton, linen, and hemp.

It's not their fault. These are perfectly good fibers, ancient and strong, that have clothed us since the early beginnings. Can the ancient inhabitants of what are now Mexico, Peru, Egypt, China, and India all have been wrong? I just prefer my fibers squishy and elastic, that's all. I like a yarn that hugs my fingers, that tugs back when I pull on it, that stretches and bends and embraces my body. A yeasted dough, only in yarn form.

Fibers grown on seed and stalk have many qualities, but bounce and elasticity are not among them. These fibers are smooth instead of curly, their internal molecules preferring a direct path to a meandering one.

The smooth nature of seed-and-stalk fibers poses few potential problems in knitting except one: When you knit a large piece of stockinette fabric and are expecting a tidy square or rectangle, you may be surprised to discover that your fabric has begun to tilt sideways, like my mother's wedding cake after its bumpy August journey across Washington, D.C., in the back of a VW Bug. It arrived the Leaning Tower of Buttercream, but artful placement of toothpicks and flowers from the garden set everything right again.

The word here is *bias*. It connotes a line that runs diagonal to the grain of a woven fabric, usually at a forty-five-degree angle. In people, it forebodes an inclination or tendency, usually erring on the side of prejudice. "I have a bias against aluminum needles," says one knitter. "I absolutely must only knit with hand-carved Burmese teak harvested sustainably by little schoolchildren." Another interrupts, "I'm biased about commercially farmed lettuce—all my greens come from a vegan farm two miles away and are delivered on horseback in hand-woven baskets."

A bias often reveals a limited worldview, a fear of the unknown or the misunderstood. The green pickup truck I spotted in Ellsworth, Maine, a few years back with a red, white, and blue bumper sticker that said, BOYCOTT FRANCE. The child who refuses to eat avocado because it's green and smooshy.

Or the knitter who refuses to try certain fibers because she's already decided she doesn't like them. I suppose if I gave them time and used them in the right context, I'd grow to love them. But I don't use them, and that's the problem.

In knitted fabric, bias exists for far simpler reasons: The yarn was given more twist than its fibers can absorb. Squishy protein fibers like wool, alpaca, and mohair are packed with zigzagging internal molecules, built-in airbags, coiled springs, and cushioned bumpers that can absorb quite a lot of force before beginning that sideways slide.

But the fibers grown from seed and stalk have no inner elasticity. While they're unflappably strong, if they fall into the company of a twist that's just a few turns too tight, they'll easily succumb to the influence. Try to knit such fibers in smooth sheets of stockinette, and, depending on the yarn and the way in which you knit, you may quickly begin to see a bias take shape.

Are these yarns innately bad? Certainly not. Nor do they deserve to be ignored as I've ignored them. Their fiber is far stronger than that of most quadrupeds, but their moral fiber simply lacks the ability to reason, to stand back and study their situation with an analytic eye, process what they're experiencing, and respond in a mature, independent manner. Instead, they feel the twist coming and raise their hands in surrender.

Having grown up in Arizona during the age of crystals and the harmonic convergence, my immediate instinct is to suggest therapy. And that's not too far off. All these fibers need is a little perspective, a 360-degree view of the situation. They need to be given a chance to pop their heads out the window and see what their own house looks like from the outside. Travel abroad. If they're in a knit stitch surrounded by other knit stitches, toss in a purl. If they're in a purl among purls, flip the working yarn back to the front and surprise them with a knit.

The mechanics of moving our yarn from one side of the fabric to the other will balance the excess twist and return the fabric to straight. It's almost as if the fibers need the contrast of knits and purls to see themselves fully, to laugh at their bias, and let it go. Worked in this way, we can still show these fibers in their full, utterly bias-free glory. It's that simple.

Of course you could go whole-hog and replace your stockinette with seed or moss stitch—the equivalent of Spanx for your fabric—or you could do something more restrained and quiet, depending on what the design dictates. But add purls, give your fabric some perspective, and your woes will disappear.

It makes me wonder. If a fabric's bias is a result of external influence, could a human's bias be similarly caused? Is it hardwired in us, this predisposition toward prejudice and foregone conclusions, or is it a response to external circumstances that we lack the ability to process? If we lack such an ability, is it permanent? Unlike the molecular structure of fibers, which is pretty hard to modify, can we actually—dare I suggest it—change? If our life is a knit stitch, what would that bias-balancing purl stitch be?

What if the BOYCOTT FRANCE guy actually went to France, spent time there, got to know the people? Would his perspective be altered, if even slightly? Does molecular change come from greater exposure to the very thing it was resisting? Can working through the wrong stitches to find the right ones help us see the world in all its glory?

I think of my nephews, two boys who are very different on the surface. The younger is outgoing and highly verbal, the older is much more quiet and contemplative. Even physically they have distinct differences. Yet the younger will do almost anything if his older brother does it. Singing a song about poop? He joins in. Suddenly likes chicken? He requests it, too. Fixated on keys? He sets off to find his own pair.

But nestled within this bias toward everything his brother does is a nascent personality of his own. I'm beginning to see it. I know that with time and a nurturing hand, that personality will develop fully, and his fabric—like my own knitting bias—will find its own way.

THE GREAT
WHODUNIT

WE ALL HAVE our coping mechanisms. I know
you're expecting me to say that mine is knitting,
and to a certain degree you'd be right. But if you
want to know the truth, my real coping mechan-
ism is a good mystery.

As far back as I can remember, mysteries have
been my favorite escape, my butterscotch sundae
with a cherry on top, a tried-and-true guilty pleasure more pleasurable, even, than holding yarn
and needles in my hands.

I come from a long line of mystery readers. My
grandma devoured them like bonbons, feasting on
the likes of Georges Simenon, Rex Stout, and, of
course, Agatha Christie. Her father-in-law preferred
his mysteries more smoky and lurid. His 1907 editions of Sherlock Holmes sit beside me even now,
their pages having been nibbled by mice last winter

to form a cozy nest in the back of the bookshelf—really a stack of old fruit crates.

There's something infinitely comforting about a good mystery. It has all the elements of great entertainment. You have a varied cast of characters, intrigue, an investigation into something gone wrong, and, ultimately, the satisfaction of a resolution. It's a puzzle, really. The story challenges you, keeps you on your guard, rewards you when you're right, leaves you gobsmacked when you're wrong, and presents brilliant twists and turns that all come together into a perfectly resolved bind-off.

The puzzle part makes me realize how much a good mystery can be like a good knitting pattern. It takes you on an adventure, engages your mind, paints a pretty landscape, maybe even surprises you now and then, but always reaches the expected resolution. It has no errata, no missing instructions, no unexpected third sleeve or illegitimate son thrown in at the end to tidy things up without regard for the original plot line.

Like writers, designers tell stories in their own way. They each have their telltale plots and characters. They employ certain kinds of charts and keys and knitting techniques, use specific language, again and again, reflecting a unique and persistent creative style across everything they do.

Long before I knew how to knit, I was already hooked on mysteries. While my brothers occupied themselves with endless games of Dungeons and Dragons, I hid out in my room and read my Hardy Boys. (No Nancy Drew for me. I got my brothers' hand-me-downs and became so fond of Frank and Joe that Nancy didn't stand a chance.)

I liked these books because you knew nothing *truly* bad was ever going to happen. No matter how high that house on the cliff or how creepy that tunnel leading to the old mill where the counterfeiters were holed up, no matter how fast the waters rushed or how loud the bad guy's gun went *bang,* you knew nobody would get killed and everything would be resolved by the last page. The best week I ever spent was at home on the couch recovering from a highly exaggerated case of the flu, with a bowl of ramen noodles, a bag of Nacho Cheese Doritos, a bottle of ginger ale, and my stack of Hardy Boys for company.

When we visited my mother's parents in the summer, I'd sleep in a tiny room under the eaves at the end of the house, with windows on three sides. It was my grandma's hideout, and in it she'd placed all of her beloved mysteries. Nothing fancy, just Bantam, Dell, and Pocket paperbacks priced at 45¢, the "newer" editions running a more decadent 60¢.

Here I met Hercule Poirot for the first time, that belovedly eccentric Belgian detective with the tidy moustache, who always referred to himself in the third person. I loved how he refused to eat two soft-boiled eggs unless they were identical in shape and size. I marveled at the way his brain seized on the most minute details—a shard of glass, a clump of garden dirt— how he always seemed to know when a postmark was genuine and when it had been altered. As great as modern television's Monk is, he has nothing on Poirot.

I jumped shelves and began reading Agatha Christie's other stories, especially those featuring Miss Marple. Far more mild-mannered and unassuming than Poirot, this innocuous little old lady had the strength to stare down the most ruthless of criminals. But her real gift was her simple ability to draw parallels between whatever she was facing at the moment and her experiences in the small town of St. Mary Mead. "It is rather reminiscent of when the spoon went missing at Hartleygate Manor," she'd say, "and everybody blamed the servant, Molly, until she finally left, and then the spoon was later found, but by then, oh, my, it was too late, now, wasn't it?"

Strangers would dismiss her talk as the random babblings of a crazy lady. But someone, somewhere, knew better. He or she did listen. And soon, as the plot unfolded, other people began to see that this woman was, in fact, more intelligent and observant than the rest of them put together. They would crane their necks for a better listen and cling to her every word. It always began with a gentle clearing of the throat, an, "Oh dear, I fear I shall explain things badly, you see, for I lack your *modern* training and all," followed by a discreet suggestion that they check behind the vicarage, or look in Lady Something-or-Other's medicine cabinet more closely. Always, the answer is there. Agatha Christie was the Elizabeth Zimmermann of the mystery world, a masterful storyteller whose language was as consistently engaging and inventive as the plots themselves. In *The Opinionated Knitter,* you can almost hear Elizabeth clearing her throat à la Miss Marple before she suggests, "There are few knitting problems that will not yield to a blend of common sense, ingenuity and resourcefulness…." I'm sure she meant to put a "my dear" in there somewhere, too.

Even my father got into the mystery game one summer

when he was living with his future in-laws down in Washington, D.C. He decided to read my grandma's entire collection of Agatha Christie books. He figured Christie *had* to have a code, some sort of secret formula she used to create her plots, and he was going to crack it once and for all.

He made it through all the books without ever figuring out her secret. But he did offer one observation. Christie was never truly sympathetic to the culprit. She'd paint pretty odious pictures of all of her characters at first—after all, that's the job of any mystery writer, to paint everybody as a suspect—but over time each person would gradually become more human, except for the true culprit, to whom Christie never showed mercy.

From Agatha Christie it was an easy leap to my grandmother's other guilty favorite, the mysteries of Georges Simenon. Suddenly we crossed the channel to a murky, gray Paris where the November cold was settling in and Inspector Maigret was hunkered in his office at the Palais de Justice, a haze of pipe smoke swirling around his head as a petty criminal squirmed in the seat across from him. Here the stories grew slightly more brutal in nature: the stabbings, the prostitutes, the severed heads. But again, the people and the environment created a vivid portrait that was as engaging as the plot itself. Paris came to life in these books, in Simenon's masterful descriptions of the streets, the smells, and, always, the food eaten by Inspector Maigret at every brasserie and bistro he passed ... they were so strikingly animated that I could almost see, smell, and taste them. And always, fairness prevailed.

Even now, the Maigret stories are my popcorn, my chaser

after a heavy meal. The summer that I was finishing up *The Knitter's Book of Wool,* my daily routine was to write all morning, have my lunch out on the porch, and then spend the rest of the afternoon tucked into a Maigret mystery. I'd blow through one book every two days, sometimes in just one day alone. It kept my mind clear, and I love thinking that perhaps a tiny bit of Maigret's Paris managed to drift in and settle among each morning's woolly words.

Many of the newer mysteries leave me cold. They seem to thrive all too often on gratuitous blood-splatters, not only telling us that the leg was severed by a chainsaw but making sure we hear the sputter of the engine and the whir of the chain as it makes its first slice into human flesh. These stories, like Stieg Larsson's Millennium trilogy, delve deep into human darkness, their conclusions reached with a realistically tired cynicism. Good may have prevailed today, but the evil and darkness lurking within each of us will ultimately win.

Thankfully, there's no blood in knitting patterns; nobody dies or loses a limb. But they can have characters who are always leaping, chasing, and being shot at. These are the knitting patterns where each row has action, your needles are performing constant acrobatics without ever getting a moment to slow down and breathe. They are packed to the gills with excess adornment, the *American Idol* contestant who insists on singing twelve trilly notes when just one steady, true one would suffice. They are laden with knitterly drama and pyrotechnics, often resulting in a spectacular garment that feels too special for everyday wear.

Other contemporary mysteries follow an even worse, cutesy "mystery lite" formula—the bulky garter-stitch scarf made out of a particularly uninventive and lifeless skein of yarn. Nothing bad happens in these books, you figure out the whole thing by page three, and then have to spend the rest of the time enduring the combative flirtings of your attractive and naturally slender heroine and Harrison, or Hadley, or Morgan, the incredibly handsome barrel-chested fire chief of her small Connecticut town.

No, for me a good mystery is the quiet kind that makes the nuance of human character an integral part of the plot. It's the knitting pattern in which yarn and stitch are kept in perfect balance. These mysteries speak to the very nature of human psychology—to the fiber itself—to who we are and what makes us do what we do. They work with yarn rather than against or in spite of it, sometimes even stepping aside so that the yarn alone can enjoy center stage.

These stories let us meet and analyze all sorts of people we'd never encounter in real life. We snoop in their drawers, we eavesdrop on their conversations, we try fabulous new stitches and techniques and materials. We're given clues and then slowly figure out who, among all these characters, would have had any reason to kill the eccentric and much-disliked master of the house. (It was the daughter-in-law. Always is.)

Agatha Christie may have kept her secrets to herself, but at a very high level, all mysteries do follow a certain formula, just as knitting patterns do. They always have the thing that happened, a murder or theft, extortion, kidnapping—a shawl, sweater, pair of mittens. They have a cast of characters, each with his or her reasons for being a likely suspect, and each with similarly compelling reasons why they couldn't possibly have done it. In knitting patterns, yarn and needles comprise your cast of characters. Our plot is the pattern itself. A good designer lays it out in a logical sequence that moves us ever forward toward resolution.

Sometimes we're led down one path that proves to be a dead end, the red herring. This is the point in our project when we realize that the instructions we've been diligently following actually had a second part that began, *"at the same time...."* None of which we'd seen or done.

By then another body is discovered, a building burned, a priceless masterpiece stolen. Our stitches look utterly peculiar, and we realize we've gotten dangerously off track. Faulty stitches fixed, we race toward the real culprit, hoping to reach him before the bind-off. Just in the nick of time, our hero or heroine figures it out. In a dramatic climax, the whole dastardly scheme is revealed and the perpetrator brought to justice. The stitches are bound off, shoulders seamed, tails darned, fabric blocked and ready to wear. The end.

Just as I've progressed from being a follower of other people's patterns to the tentative creator of my own, I've also started to dabble in writing my own mysteries. I keep them in a notebook I've jokingly titled *The Knitter's Book of Plots.* Just as I have no illusions of being a fabulous knitwear designer, these stories need work. But the act of writing a plot is a great mental game. Like swatching, it lets you establish your gauge and piece together all sorts of scenarios, figuring out the what-ifs until everything makes sense, your numbers match, your plot is foolproof. You can do all of this without ever having to follow through and cast on a single stitch or write a word of dialogue. Some of the best patterns were conceived on paper before any stitch was knit. Of course, some of the worst patterns were conceived this way, too.

There are good mysteries and bad mysteries, good patterns and bad ones and *truly* ghastly ones. A bad mystery is enough to put you off mysteries forever, just as a bad pattern can send you off your knitting for a good long while. The lousy mystery leaves ends undarned. Its plot is flawed. The characters may be weak, their behavior not always consistent; the yarn is a poor match for what the pattern is asking of it. The writer omits crucial facts. The conclusion was reached too hastily, the hem of your sleeve is far shorter than any human arm would ever be. You're left scratching your head when the pattern later instructs you to pick up the stitches that you'd placed on the holder. What holder? What stitches?

The very worst of the lot are those that end by revealing a *new* undarned end, a shadowy figure shaking his fist and shouting, "I'll get you for this!" before slipping away into the bushes. Advertising a sequel to badness is unconscionable.

But the good mystery? You're sad to bind off and eager for the next adventure. Once you stumble onto a designer and designs you like, you'll knit anything they put out. You derive comfort and inspiration from their creative process. You might even spend a whole summer trying to decipher *their* formula.

AUNT JUDY

EVERYBODY HAS AN Aunt Judy. That may not be her actual name, but we all have that one aunt we especially adore—the one who was there for us in ways our parents couldn't be, who loved us unconditionally, and whose house was the greatest place on earth to visit. You know the Aunt Judy I'm talking about. What was yours named?

Mine really is an Aunt Judy. She's my father's oldest sister, and she lives in Michigan with my Uncle Russ in a yellow house with porches on all sides, surrounded by a garden more overrun and magical than the one in the children's book by Frances Hodgson Burnett.

We used to visit Aunt Judy often. I associate her with laughter, playing in the pool, eating ice cream, running around barefoot. There was a complete lack of drama around Aunt Judy, just pure, unadulterated childhood happiness—even when her Saint Bernard, Toby, fell in love with my mother and had to be locked in the basement.

Aunt Judy was a schoolteacher, and she spent every spare minute out in her garden. Her parents were passionate gardeners, and she shared their fascination with all things green. She dutifully planted her yard according to a plan her father had drawn for her. After he died, she and my grandmother traveled the world visiting gardens. She's a master gardener and can tell you the Latin name of almost any plant—and not in that snub "watch me speak Latin" way, but more like a kid who's showing her favorite toys to a friend.

My brothers would always run off with her son, Roger, and do older "boy" things together. I worshipped her daughter, Kathy, who was also older than me. In her I had an actual friend, a girl with whom I could stay up late having whispered conversations in the dark. The year Kathy redecorated her room with jet-black carpet, silver wallpaper, and matching silver Venetian blinds, my brain nearly exploded from awe. My parents' divorce made our visits less frequent, and soon our age difference broke the spell. She started working in the summers and then moved into her own apartment. We visited her there, but it wasn't the same.

Once I reached my twenties, I didn't see my aunt or my cousin very often. And I certainly didn't reveal many of the exciting upheavals in my life. We wrote Christmas cards and kept the conversation light, but when Clare and I made our cross-country move to Maine, we made a pilgrimage to Aunt Judy's house. She welcomed us with open arms.

I used to think that my knitting lineage could only be traced back through my mother's side of the family to my grandma, but late in her life I learned that my "other" grandma—Aunt Judy's mother, who insisted on being called "Grandmother"— also knew how to knit.

She was a violinist, and her husband was a composer and conductor. They met at the Eastman School of Music, the same school where my parents met some thirty years later. When they were first married, my grandfather arranged music for Buffalo Bill's radio program and my grandmother played violin in the Buffalo Philharmonic. This was in the early 1930s, when women rarely worked outside of the home, and they *certainly* didn't perform in orchestras. She was one of the few women who did, and she later spent thirty-seven years as concert-mistress of the Battle Creek Symphony Orchestra.

But back in Buffalo during rehearsals, the conductor some-times focused on one part of a piece, leaving several of the musicians twiddling their thumbs. My grandmother used the time to pull out a tiny sweater she was working on, presum-ably for my aunt, and sneak in a few rows. But the conductor noticed. He glared at her, and then her knitting, until finally she put it away. After the rehearsal, the conductor came over. "Mrs. Parkes," he said in a heavy Hungarian accent, "What were you doing just now?"

Before she could answer, he began to critique her knitting. Not that she was *knitting,* but that her *technique* was wrong. He grabbed her sweater and promptly began demonstrating the "proper" way to knit.

She gave up knitting not too long after that. It didn't give her nearly the pleasure that playing violin and puttering in the dirt did. A year after my grandmother passed away, Aunt Judy decided to come to a knitting retreat I was putting together in Virginia. She seemed a little untethered by her loss, as if she'd lost the "tock" to her "tick." Try as she may, her daughter, Kathy, just couldn't share in her mother's love of gardening. Her thumb was not green at all, and I know she felt bad about this, as if she were letting her mother down. But Kathy *was* intrigued by knitting and by the prospect of getting to see me. She asked her mother if she could come along.

"Of course you can," said Aunt Judy. "But you realize you'll have to learn how to knit?" A minor detail.

On an airplane headed east from Detroit, at an altitude of approximately 35,000 feet, my Aunt Judy put knitting needles in Kathy's hands for the first time. She had no reason to like it, especially since she'd been given a bent pair of scratched aluminum Susan Bates needles and a frayed, pilly old ball of synthetic yarn. Yet Kathy took to knitting like a fish to water.

My Aunt Judy hadn't knit since her kids were young, so her technique was, like her own needles, a little rough around the edges. Every few rows, the empty needle would slip from her hand and hit the classroom's linoleum floor with such a clatter that everyone would stop what they were doing and stare. It was such an effective attention-getter that it became our official gavel, gong, and dinner bell. "Where's Aunt Judy?" I'd ask, and then patiently wait for her to finish her row before taking her needle.

Aunt Judy and Kathy fell in love with knitting together. They quickly replaced those old aluminum needles with fresh new ones. They took classes and made road trips to farms and yarn stores. Between them, they began amassing quite a collection of yarn. By the next year's retreat, Aunt Judy was doing colorwork and Kathy was putting zippers in vests. They haven't missed a year since.

That first retreat took place at Graves Mountain Lodge, an old-fashioned family inn tucked in the foothills of the Shenandoah National Park and the Blue Ridge Mountains. Each morning, we'd leave the inn buildings and smaller cottages and wander downhill to the main lodge for a gigantic meal, served family style, before beginning our classes. Everything was canned or fried, and nearly every dish had apples in it, apples being Graves Mountain's main agricultural export.

The three of us, Aunt Judy and Kathy and I, were in a small cottage at the top of the hill, just beyond the upper apple orchards where bears hung out. Our cabin had a big stone fireplace and was crawling with Asian lady beetles—which, under the right circumstances, can pass for the more charming ladybugs. From a rocking chair on the back porch, you could watch the sun rise across the valley.

Each night, Kathy and I lay in our respective twin beds, listening to the occasional buzz and thud of the "ladybugs," whispering to one another until we fell asleep. That first year I had a momentary flash of my grandmother smiling down upon us from her cloud. She was a little bemused at what her daughter and granddaughters were doing—so unlike anything that had given *her* pleasure—but so pleased that we were all together. In fact, I think she was nodding to herself, as if this were the permission she needed in order to move on.

Today, Kathy's daughter Kaitlyn is starting to make noise about coming to the retreat, too. I don't think she has any particular passion for knitting yet, she just wants to be a part of the tradition and help carry it forward.

With no children of my own, I have nobody to whom I can pass on my knitting tradition. But I've done a few things of which I'm particularly proud—I've kept an old farmhouse from falling down for another generation, I've written some books that I hope have been helpful to knitters. And I've been able to keep the knitting genes alive and strong within other branches of my family tree. While my two nephews show no inclination toward yarn, my niece, Emma, *did* finger-knit a mile of acrylic last summer. There may still be hope after all.

COMING UNDONE

I HAVE A FAVORITE Robert Frost saying that comforts me, even though it's been co-opted by many self-help books: "There's no way out but through." We have to walk through an experience. We can't avoid or bypass life's journey. We can't cop out, numb out, or simply fast-forward.

Moving through something involves a progression of steps, of putting one foot in front of the other. Even if you drive, you have to travel the distance between here and there. Wish as I may, we haven't yet figured out a way to fold up the world into an accordion-style map and hop over the folds to reach our destination faster.

Sequential processes often have very good reasons for being ordered as they are. We make cakes in a certain order so that the ingredients can respond to one another. Dry is usually sifted with dry, moist with moist. We're told to whip the butter and sugar together—not just so it looks pretty, but so that when the batter heats up, each sugar crystal will melt and release tiny pockets of moisture that give that perfect crumb. We're told to add flavoring agents like vanilla to the butter mixture not just because they're both rather wet but because fat is an excellent carrier for flavor. In sequential tasks, everything has a reason and order to it.

Think of knitting. It's the ultimate sequential task. You can't reach your destination—a finished garment—without walking each step, forming each stitch along the way. You can speed it up by using bigger needles or a knitting machine. But even then, each stitch still has to exist, the increases and decreases alike. You can't knit a neckline until you've reached the neck. You'll have something, but it certainly won't be a neckline.

Knitting does, however, offer a rare opportunity that few other sequential activities do. It lets us hit the "undo" button and start over without there being any permanent damage. There's nothing to throw out, no paper to crumple and toss in the trash, no spoiled batter or ugly canvas. Sure, there's no way out of a sweater except to knit it. But if you look closely, you'll actually see an open window: If our knitting is not working, we can simply slide our needles out of the fabric, tug at the end of our yarn, unravel the stitches, and hop out.

This undoing of knitting has a nickname. We call it "frogging" because we're ripping out our stitches, muttering "rip-it, rip-it," like the call of a frog. Frogs are great creatures. Their presence reassures us that our wetlands are still healthy. Their springtime evening calls fill the air with sounds of love and the promise of a summer to come. A single kiss and, poof, you may suddenly be face-to-face with the prince or princess of your dreams. Kiss a ball of yarn? Nothing. I've tried.

The literal-minded will raise their eyebrow, reminding us that stitches don't actually make a *rip-it* sound as they're being undone, nor do most of us mutter those words when undoing our stitches. At least I don't. (The words I mumble aren't suitable for publication.) Nothing is being ripped, which would imply a sustained tearing apart. Still, *frog* has been widely adopted because it lends a whimsical, cheerful perspective to unravelling, an act that holds much more negative baggage.

Nothing good comes to those who unravel. Have you ever noticed? We read about the woman who wakes up one day and hacks her family into tiny pieces, puts arsenic in the church coffee pots, fills her pockets with stones and walks into the sea.

Things, too, come unraveled. Hems, marriages, businesses, economies, and entire nations alike have met equally dramatic demises. There's not much positive imagery associated with the word *unravel*. Look it up in the dictionary, and you'll see definitions like "to come undone" or "to fail." No wonder we prefer the croak of a tailless amphibian.

Coming unraveled may connote losing it, but sometimes it's best to acknowledge with quite a level head that something you thought was right isn't, that you need to undo as best you can and rebuild. In life, you can't start from scratch as a baby and relive your days differently. But in knitting—most knitting anyway—you can. If you're patient, you can pull your yarn out of whatever mess you may have gotten it into. You can hit "rewind," literally rewinding the yarn back to its beginning.

In my sophomore year of college, I had my own personal unraveling of sorts. I couldn't put my finger on it exactly, but I felt as if my life was out of control. I'd been so good at being the person I thought other people wanted me to be—the good daughter, the honor student, the model employee—yet I couldn't find any actual *me* in there. I was losing it.

By some stroke of luck, I found a smart, skilled woman with whom I met for an hour each week to sort things out. It was a slow process, at times tedious and painful, other times funny and enlightening. Ever so gradually, we began to sort through the mess and figure out who Clara really was. It was the most helpful thing I've ever done.

Therein lies the mystery of unraveling. Dig a little deeper in the dictionary, and you'll notice that *unravel* also means to loosen, to disentangle, or to solve, as when Miss Marple unraveled the mystery of the body in the library. We may be physically undoing one thing, but we're solving something bigger. We're untangling a problem, loosening a situation that may have become too tight, too restrictive to our creativity. It's not all bad; in fact quite the opposite. Unraveling can be a blessing.

As we're undoing all that hard work, we're also wiping the slate clean, resetting the odometer. We're another day older and wiser, with a ball of slightly kinked but perfectly good yarn to show for it. If we're lucky, we have a greater sense of perspective on what got us into this mess in the first place and how we can avoid it next time.

MAKING MARTHA'S SANDWICH

EVERY MAINE TOWN has a market, the epicenter
of the community, a spiritual and commercial hub.
Need to know anything about anything at all—
who died, who's sleeping with whom, whose barn
fell down—go there.

Mine is the Buck's Harbor Market. It was Eddie's
Market when I was growing up, Eddie being a jolly
fellow who gave me free licorice while keeping a
heavy thumb on the scale. One year he made a pretty
penny by freezing snow and selling it as "genuine
authentic Maine snowballs" to the summer tourists.

Something is always happening at the market.
In years past, radio correspondent Allie Furlaud
could be found shouting into the pay phone over an
idling Coke truck as she filed a report. "I'm trying
to talk to Paris!" she would yell to a driver who, in
true Maine fashion, would simply blink at her

and continue about his business. One foggy morning I just missed Teddy Kennedy, who'd moored in the harbor and come up for supplies. "Only a goddamned fool would be out on a day like this," muttered one of the town gossips, nursing a Styrofoam cup of coffee nearby.

Eddie is long gone but the spirit of the market endures, and I'm accustomed to being greeted with a challenge when I stop by. Sometimes I'm asked for a ride to Portland, or to water someone's garden for a few days, or for advice on how to start an alpaca farm or block a shawl. I never know. So I wasn't at all surprised the day I walked in and was offered a chance to make a sandwich for Martha Stewart.

She was in town filming a segment of her TV show with Eliot Coleman, our prominent four-season organic gardener, author, and television personality. Her entourage had probably driven right by my house that morning. Did she notice my blooming rugosa hedge? Yikes, did she *tsk tsk* at my leaning mailbox or the peeling paint under the eaves?

One of her assistants had called in a lunch order, and everyone was in a tizzy. Nobody wanted to be responsible for her sandwich. Before I had a chance to decide, Butch, the market's convivial owner, shook his head. "Oh, you guys," he sighed, "I'll make it." He wandered over to the deli case and pulled out a tube of liverwurst. The domestic maven whose net worth at that time was over $1 billion had ordered a liverwurst sandwich.

Truth is, I would've loved to do it. But I'm left only with the memory of the day I *almost* got to make Martha Stewart a liverwurst sandwich.

There's something about being by the ocean, witnessing its regular flushing of the tide, that makes you feel like change is always afoot. Beneath the hats, behind the sunglasses, under the shadow of sails, you never know who's out there—or who's waving to you from shore. Mingled among the working lobstermen, you might see Martha and her shiny $1 million Hinckley Picnic Boat, or a regatta from the New York Yacht Club, or a pair of sea kayaks (the lobstermen call them "speed bumps") paddling from cove to cove. Could be anyone.

Dan Fogelberg used to sail to and fro between our side of the bay and his home on Deer Isle. Robert McCloskey motored by with his daughters on journeys similar to the one he narrated in his children's classic *One Morning in Maine*. And E.B. White was a fixture, sailing up and down Eggemoggin Reach within a slingshot's reach of my own rocks.

Whoever it is—strangers from all walks of life—you pass, smile, wave, and move on. If it's a particularly beautiful boat, you add a thumbs-up to your wave. Passing close, you might yell, "Looking good!"

The ocean even launched my grandfather in his career. He was moored in Bucks Harbor, and another boat moored nearby. A conversation ensued about something random and boat-related, I'm sure. The sailor was, like my young grandfather, rather quiet and soft-spoken, a bit of a geek. It turned out he was director of research at the Naval Research Laboratory. My grandfather ended up spending most of his career at that laboratory, with this man as his mentor. All that from one chance encounter on a boat.

I didn't take to sailing nearly as quickly as I took to knitting. My grandma showed me the knit stitch, and it was off to the races. The water part was trickier. I love every part of swimming, but the minute my parents put me on a sailboat, I became the screaming kid who makes everyone miserable. When I felt the boat tip and my center of gravity shift, I was convinced the whole boat was seconds away from capsizing and dragging us all down, down, down, to our dark, watery graves. It didn't help that we kept our boat in Deadman's Cove.

When I moved back to Maine as an adult, I spent my first few summers on shore, waving wistfully to the sailboats from under my big floppy hat. They looked so graceful and inviting—if only I could be on one of them. I signed up for a sailing class at the nearby WoodenBoat School, and after more than twenty years of saying no, I accepted an invitation to sail on *Fledgling*.

In the boating world, the name of a boat is often better known than that of its owners. *Fledgling* is one such vessel. This hundred-year-old wooden sailboat has been a fixture in my ominously named cove forever. Early home movies of us getting into our own sailboat (me already crying) reveal the elegant outlines of *Fledgling* in the distance. If wooden boats were instruments, this one would be a Stradivarius.

My friend Don grew up sailing the bay in *Fledgling* with his father. If a rock could be hit at low tide, they hit it. As a teenager, he sanded and varnished nearly every piece of wood, tied every rope, polished every cleat. He knows this boat like the back of his hand and could sail it in his sleep.

Don is now in his eighties, though spiritually he's still a

robust twenty-four. Until a few years ago, he went sailing alone. On sunny afternoons, he'd strip naked, letting the cockpit (pardon the pun) conceal his nether parts from passersby. One day, he had the brilliant idea of bringing his new miniature schnauzer, Annie, with him. Barking at the waves, she lost her balance and fell in. Don loosened all the ropes and jumped in after her, but one of the ropes got caught. As he reached her, he turned around just in time to see his beautiful *Fledgling* sailing away. A nearby motorboat had witnessed the whole thing and came to his rescue—pulling a completely naked Don out of the water. I believe that was the last time he sailed in the nude, or with a miniature schnauzer.

Everything I didn't learn at WoodenBoat School I learned from Don. He has a gentle, wise disposition that I can trust on the water. His partner, Robert, has a more mischievous, dare I say pragmatic side. On our first sail, Don reassured me everything would be fine, while Robert counseled that death by drowning is the best way to go. But Don was right, everything *was* fine, and it continues to be every time we go out on the water.

I approached my first turned heel with a similar sense of both terror and disbelief—although, let's be real, I don't know of anybody dying from a heel-turning accident. Still, the heel looked so complicated, so architectural and shapely. Worked in the round, no less, it couldn't *possibly* be easy. I was following the simplest pattern ever written, yet even that pattern's heel instructions had so many rows, so many numbers, so many *do-this, do-thats.* Turn your work. Now do this, but not exactly like you did last time. Then do that, but at a slightly different place. Turn your work. *Pay attention! Don't look out the window!* Too late. It's all ruined.

I remember clinging to those instructions as if they were my lifejacket in a boat doomed to sink. With each row, I saw only impending disaster. Eventually I'd reached the point of no return, well beyond a swimmable distance to shore. Going back would be just as terrifying, so I stuck it out in the hopes that my sock would live to see the end. Now, many more heels later, I've realized just how simple and intuitive heels really are. All I needed to do was relax, take a deep breath, and keep the big picture in sight. Needles find their way, boats are built to float, and it's often our *mind* that is our worst enemy. These days, when Don calls with an invitation to sail on *Fledgling*, I drop everything, grab my life jacket, and go—just as when certain designers publish new patterns, I drop whatever's on my needles and cast on anew.

Both sailing and knitting were once essential components of everyday life, now relegated somewhat to the realm of "esoteric"—along with the record player and fountain pen—by such modern inventions as the combustion engine and the knitting machine. And yet how exquisite they both are.

When you sail, you're gliding through water, propelled only by the wind and an artfully slanted sail. Everything is silent except for the sound of wind and water, and perhaps the slight creaking of your boat. If you're lucky, a harbor seal will pop up its head and watch you go by. In the middle of my bay, the air smells sweet—so sweet I make myself dizzy trying to breathe it all in. I've been passed by monarch butterflies and circled by a pod of porpoises; I've sideswiped driftwood and trailed my fingers in the water while feeling overwhelmed by the perfection of the moment.

Knitting offers a quieter, dare I say drier escape into that zone. We still the mind and let our fingers maneuver yarn over, under, through, and off a needle, again and again. How utterly simple those movements, yet, lo, is that fabric I see? Yes. Lovely, durable, beautiful, functional fabric unfolds before us. Just from wiggling our fingers.

The lapping of the waves against our needles is a whisper, a sliding of crimp and scales, of compressed energy and twist, against a solid surface. Wooden needles bring choppy waters, our boat fighting against the current. We glide faster with metal needles, interrupted only by the occasional *tink tink tink* of metal on metal, like steel-masted sailboats rocking in the harbor. Occasionally we are greeted by a passerby: a fleck of vegetation, a variation in twist, a knot perhaps. We greet it and move on, ever forward, plowing through wave after wave of stitches on our way to a distant point, a sleeve, a sock.

All too often I meet a person who says she knows how to knit, but then quickly adds, "But I'm not, you know, a *real* knitter." Hooey. Neither materials nor output do a knitter make. You can own a $100,000 wooden Concordia yawl and easily be outmaneuvered by an amateur at the tiller of a friend's little boat (ask me how I know). On a windy day, you could even hold up a bedsheet in a borrowed canoe and have a blast.

Knitters, whether you make museum-quality creations out of your own handspun Mongolian cashmere or garter-stitch washcloths out of cotton, you, too, can have a blast. You don't need fancy-pants needles (nothing against them) or fancy-pants yarn (nothing against it) or a fancy-pants project (you know where this is going) to enjoy yourself and to be, in every sense of the word, a knitter.

And despite her 35,000-square-foot vacation home just up the coast, Martha understands this, too. Why else, when the media mogul was presented with a humble acrylic poncho crocheted by a fellow inmate on the eve of her release, would she proudly wear it out into the free world? Never before—and probably never again—has a poncho made such a big stir.

Which is why I'm confident she would've appreciated my liverwurst sandwich. *Psssst, Martha, call me.*

HAPPILY
EVER AFTER

I LIVE IN A farmhouse on a bluff of a peninsula looking inland across blueberry fields, treetops, and water
to rolling, rocky hills that eventually lead to Canada.
My view is unmarred by any human structure save
for the distant blinking of cell phone towers.

The house was built in the typical New England
style, with a big house leading to a middle house, to
an unfinished back house, and finally to a barn. The
big house was built in 1893, with the middle, back,
and barn built soon after. I like to think that most of
the trim came from the Sears Roebuck catalog.

The view called to Clare and me during a brief
visit in the summer of 1995. We were exploring the
perimeter of my Great-Aunt Kay's house, long since
boarded up and uninhabited. We pushed our way
through the bamboo, the sumac, the tall, forbidding
weeds doing their best to keep us back. When we

finally reached the north side of the house, we discovered three windows at waist height, which had not been boarded up or covered from the inside. I cupped my hands to the glass and peered in, seeing a small sitting room with two rocking chairs. It had all sorts of garbage piled high, but I remember the rocking chairs.

As if on cue, both of us followed the gaze of whoever would have been sitting in those chairs. It was not the view I normally saw from the road when driving by her house. It was a far more settled, perfect, painterly landscape, a siren's call to my city-weary soul. Suddenly I saw myself in that room, cleaned and lovingly brought back to life again, sitting in one of those rocking chairs and gazing out at that view. I knew, without a doubt, that this was where we were meant to be.

That week we hatched a plot, which we jokingly called "Operation Freedom." We would find a way to leave San Francisco, move to Maine, transform that farmhouse into our very own home, and live happily ever after.

Everyone thought we were crazy. On the outside, the house was a disaster. Peeling paint, cracked plaster, windows that barely held their glass in place. A few years earlier, the first floor had given up completely and rotted into the muddy basement, taking all its belongings with it. The floor had been rebuilt and some possessions put back in place, but the rest was still heaped in the barn.

The house was like the remains of a fine sweater discovered quite by accident in an old, forgotten suitcase. Moths had eaten through the stitches. Both elbows had blown through, wrists were worn away, the shoulders thinned to a shadow of their former selves. But the compassionate eye saw potential. All the original lines were still there, the granite foundation and steady roofline signaling, unquestionably, possibility.

My great-aunt was a character deserving of a book all her own. Immediately after World War II, she traveled throughout Europe for the Audubon Society presenting a film on the birds of North America. She cared for her ailing parents, never marrying or having children of her own. When her parents died, she took on the responsibility of caring for their belongings—and they had many, for they'd never been able to part with what they'd inherited from *their* parents' houses. The family home was jammed with generations and generations of things that held no real appeal to an outsider. When prompted, she would launch into a story about how so-and-so, from somewhere-or-other, used this for something a long, long time ago.

Perhaps she noticed that we were bored senseless by these stories, my brothers and I, for she began writing them down on pale yellow tags and affixing them to things—"Key to Arthur Cyrus Hill's office, dentist, Boston, 1843," read one, or "Sterling spoons marked ARH, gift to Adella Richards Hill from Emma Aline Osgood, Somerville, 1861." Naturally, my brothers and I responded by adding our own labels to things. "Spatula, handle partially melted by Jeffrey Tousey Parkes, Maine, 1984," with the name underlined three times for emphasis.

Aunt Kay was a true eccentric who followed her own compass and didn't care what anyone said or thought. To her, it was only natural that the passenger's seat of her car should be removed, so that her dog, Loki, could get in and out more easily. Today, she might have been featured on *Hoarders,* but she was, in kinder terms, a curator of the world's abandoned belongings. The fact that some of those things came from the dump was really beside the point. She was saving treasures that others had so carelessly left behind.

We didn't get the keys to her farmhouse until a year after we arrived in Maine. We'd spent that first year in Portland getting our footing, Clare finding work and me building my freelance career, both of us ecstatically noting things like The First Firefly, The First Snowfall, and The First Power Outage.

When we finally got inside the farmhouse, the scope of our folly hit home. The place was a wreck. Broken chairs, rusty box springs, parlor pianos (yes, plural), a roll of used fiberglass insulation, stacks of green window shutters that did not belong to the house, two kerosene-filled oil drums that sprang a leak as we rolled them out. There were steamer trunks jammed with mildewed sheets and moth-eaten blankets that had been home to generations of squirrels and mice. We leafed through heaps of old navigational charts Aunt Kay's parents had used when cruising up the coast from Boston to Maine each summer. It was as if every stitch in the sweater had been somehow compromised. What had once passed for a kitchen pantry now held serving platters and rusty paint cans alike. And there were stoves. Gas stoves from the 1960s, cast-iron stoves from the 1800s. We counted twenty-four total, only two of which were fully functioning. Stoves were her favorite. When I once asked why, she answered, "Why not?"

We took a full year to empty out the farmhouse, driving up each Friday night, working all weekend, and schlepping our exhausted selves back home on Sunday evening. It's a miracle neither of us contracted hantavirus because the whole upstairs was one giant fossilized pile of mouse and bat dung. Yet the house still called to us, so we toiled, investing every penny we had to bring this old place back to life.

So vast were the needed repairs, and so limited our skills, that we hired someone to manage the work for us. He would oversee the stripping of the house down to its very joists, patching, rewiring, restoring, insulating, replacing windows, installing heat and bathrooms and a functioning kitchen where none had existed for decades. My goal was to breathe new life back into this house while making any upgrades invisible to the passerby. I wanted it to stay as true to the original sweater design as possible, to look like nothing but a farmhouse that had been lovingly tended all these years. I'd salvage what I could, gently tease apart what I couldn't, then spin, dye, and slowly reknit.

In the beginning, I adored the process of rebuilding this house, marking the exact spot for each electrical outlet, lightbulb, and switch. Each room was positioned to maximize a specific view I'd imagined in my head. Everything, down to the last hinge and doorknob, existed for a reason.

I was designing what I envisioned would be the perfect sweater, one that matched every contour of our bodies so completely that we'd never need another sweater, ever again. All this was on paper and in my imagination. As it gradually transformed into the three-dimensional reality of a home, the disappointments came. Stitches didn't resemble what I'd imagined, rows had decreases that didn't match the perfect slant I'd drawn on graph paper. Original window hardware was thrown away by mistake, a beautiful old attic window was broken by one of the workers. Why hadn't they vented the stove the way I'd asked? Shouldn't this outlet be a quad?

The longer the project lingered, the less fuss I made when things weren't right. When bathroom fixtures arrived without my ever having specified them, I gave up. I'd reached that point in the project where I was sick of everything. I just wanted to bind off the damned stitches and finally wear the sweater. So what if the cuff was too loose? I could always unravel that part and redo it later, right?

As anyone who's renovated an old farmhouse will confirm, the project took twice as long and cost twice as much as estimated. We were out of money and beginning to compromise with the game of "I'll give you X if you'll still do Y." Now in play were two crucial pieces: the porch and the septic system.

One reason I rebuilt the farmhouse was so that we could put a screened porch off the back and live in it all summer long, gazing out at that amazing view without ever having to slap a mosquito. But we'd become so bogged down with matters of insulation and windows and heating systems, the contractor's unraveling marriage and his foreman's drinking problem, that the porch was now on the chopping block. If the septic tank was compromised in any way—and all signs pointed to "yes"—the porch would have to go. Everything else, in fact, would need to be cut.

Our local plumber, Bobby Gray, is related to half the town and has probably been in every house at one point or another. He told me he'd installed the original tank in 1976. Remembered it as if it were yesterday. (Most people who'd had dealings with Kay did not easily forget her.) It was a steel tank—he even knew the gallon size—and it had to be rusted through by now. There's no way a tank could last that long, he said.

When they began to dig where Bobby had said it was, they found nothing. They kept digging and digging, until suddenly they hit something hard. It didn't make a metallic bang but more of a dense, tomblike thud. The sound of hitting concrete.

I don't know how she did it, but my perfectly eccentric Great-Aunt Kay had managed to install an entirely new septic system in her back field without anyone in my town of 910 taking notice. I call it the Miracle of the Septic Tank, and to this day I give thanks to what I can only assume was the work of a benevolent Saint Septius. It was like discovering a stash of pristine leftover yarn, not only in the same color but the very same *dye lot* we needed. Our sweater could now be finished, trim and button bands, porch and septic alike.

The week before a family reunion was to take place in my town, and where I was to preview our nearly finished masterpiece, I got a call. There had been a fire. Everything was done—the heat, the insulation, the walls, the windows, the roof—and we were in the home stretch, refinishing the wide pine floor boards. The refinisher had left his debris in a black plastic bag in the corner of a sunny bay window. The heat of the sun caused the materials in the bag to combust, smoldering through two layers of floor and into the basement. When our foreman arrived, unusually early and totally by chance, the fire had just burned through to the outside wall, where the added oxygen would have surely brought the whole house down in a matter of minutes. He hooked up a garden hose and sprayed until the volunteer fire department, led by our neighbor three houses up, could arrive.

It had never occurred to either of us that we'd lose the house before ever getting to live in it. But after the initial shock, we both realized that we felt strangely okay about the whole thing, like losing our dream wasn't the end of the journey at all.

Finally, on a brisk October day, the very minute it was deemed ready, we moved in, sweeping out the last of the workers and locking the door behind us. Every wall, door, and linear foot of trim still needed painting, but no matter. We were finally wearing the sweater of our dreams, and life was good.

I'll admit it now, we could've done a better job preserving the original yarn. Our neighbor Wayne, a robust eighty-nine at the time, presented us with a housewarming gift: a box of perfectly cut kindling made from the discarded laths that had been heaped out front. I cannot bear to burn these pieces of wood, they are such a beauty—as if Wayne had taken the very fibers from the moth-eaten parts I'd rejected and patiently respun them into tidy little skeins for darning. They sit in their box, which he'd covered with recycled Christmas paper, as reminders to us both to look twice before discarding anything.

I love my farmhouse. It is the closest thing to "home" I've managed to create for myself. I know its smells and sounds, I can navigate it in the dark. Walls and trim that were brand new with the renovation now have cracks and dings and smudges all their own. The tender pink bricks of the newly laid fireplace are now well-seasoned from years of quiet, contented evenings gazing at the embers. Far from "done," it remains a work in progress, rather like life itself.

Everyone thought we'd moved to the middle of nowhere, but that's the irony. I'm surrounded by people. They're quirky, a little rough around the edges, but also kind, clever, and resourceful. They're welcoming and accepting without any sense of self-awareness. A few travel back and forth by private jet, building their own outdoor elevators so they can reach their yachts without having to climb stairs. But when asked, they also used their money to buy the local market when it risked closing, running it at a financial loss and with immeasurable benefit to the community.

My other neighbors (the ones without the jets) are always busy. They're cutting firewood in the winter, setting out their lobster traps, planting seedlings, shooting deer. They tend to their children, grandchildren, and gardens, their kitchens always steaming with canning activity every August. They also socialize. They gather at the market. They hold protest signs, bring casseroles to the hungry, and sing together on Sunday.

Ask almost anyone in my little town, and they'll agree that it's as close to paradise as you can get. But you know what? Given the opportunity, almost everybody who can afford it leaves for a little while. Especially in the winter.

Helen and Scott Nearing were once neighbors. These famous homesteaders and organic farmers proudly lived off the land. But they, too, would quietly slip away to sunnier climates in the dead of winter. As I write this, the Nearing's protégée Eliot Coleman and his wife, Barbara Damrosch, are sunning themselves at an eco-tourism resort in Argentina.

Absence makes the heart grow fonder. I certainly appreciate my little town more after I've been away. The closer we get to home, the more alert and excited I become, like a dog who knows he's going to his favorite beach. My nose perks up. I open the windows so I can smell the fresh air. The road gets narrower and bumpier and windier, the sights more familiar until, finally, I'm on roads I could travel in my sleep. We pull into our driveway, stop the engine, and sit still for a minute to take it all in. The silence unfolds around us, then the other sounds: the far-off bell buoy in the harbor, the flickering of leaves, the hermit thrush singing from deep in the woods. In the spring, the sudden intensity of peepers.

My little corner of Maine is where I feel closest to God—the creator, benevolent spirit, whatever you'd like to call it—and for this I gave up a prosperous career in the most beautiful city in the world, a place where roses grow year-round, jobs are plentiful, and public transportation is easy and abundant. I gave it all up, and my life has been unimaginably richer for it.

But it's not perfectly rosy. We haven't yet figured out how to make a living selling blueberries by the side of the road, so we still spend part of each week several hours away from our beloved farmhouse in the not-so-grand metropolis of Portland. Clare goes there to work, I go there to be in the world.

It's taken me a while to accept the fact that my dream

sweater isn't enough. It turns out I also need people, energy, vibrancy, and community, more than my town of 910 can provide. I crave variety, that grain of sand in my oyster, the daily walk through Mr. Rogers's busy little neighborhood. I like to greet the tattooed man with his tiny dog, pass the elderly couple waiting for the bus, smile to the guy who's always standing in front of the gay bar, morning cigarette in one hand, coffee mug in the other, who tells me the doctor told him to stop but what the hell, he'll die happy. I love to be greeted by name at my coffee place and presented with a cappuccino with a perfectly formed heart in its foam.

It turns out, "happily ever after" is a moving target. No matter how perfect any one sweater may be, it's only human to crave another. And another, and another.

ACKNOWLEDGMENTS

Writing a book is a lot like knitting a sweater. To the casual observer, it looks like just one person wiggling fingers over needles or a keyboard. This can go on for months, years even, before the end result is proudly worn into the world, the maker's name squarely on the cover. What looks like a solitary endeavor is, in fact, supported at every step by a broad foundation of people.

"Do you like this stitch?" or "Is this dreadfully boring?" we ask a trusted few, those we know will encourage the good and warn us away from the unflattering. I am grateful to my friends and trusted readers, especially to Jane, Jen, and Cat, for helping me sort through all the swatches and find the right stitch, gauge, and pattern for this book.

The writer, like the wool in our yarn, is the product of generations upon generations of breeding, prudent upbringing, and careful finishing. Here I must thank my family, both past and present, for existing exactly as they were and are, and for allowing me to tell my side of our collective stories here. I come from good stock, creative, bright, and occasionally eccentric people who all share common traits of large foreheads and a penchant for puns.

The agent acts as a compass for our lone writer as she navigates that sea of stitches. Elizabeth Kaplan served as my advocate, negotiator, idea-bouncer-offer, and respected compatriot. There was not a moment when I didn't feel she had my back.

Not that she needed to, because I was in good hands. Melanie Falick is the writer's editor, the kind I thought only existed at places like *The New Yorker*. To be able to conceive of this book and bring it to fruition in her partnership has been a gift.

Then there's the long-suffering partner. Clare lived most intimately with this project. She has endured hours of conversation about something that, let's be honest, wasn't always that interesting. Writing is a solitary act, and the writer mid-book can be dreadful company. Before the chapters came together as a whole, before any sign of a sweater was there, Clare nodded and smiled, read those lousy first drafts, brought mug after mug of tea, and never faltered in saying, "You can do it." I can't possibly put my gratitude into words, I can only repay the debt with a lifetime supply of fresh-baked biscuits and the promise that I'll do all the Christmas shopping, wrapping, and shipping from now to eternity.

And you, my dear reader? I wrote this book for you. I wasn't able to take your measurements or ask, "Would you prefer red or blue?" But I worked each stitch with a mental picture of you. I carried you with me, and you were fine company. You laughed at the funny parts, shook your head when I strayed. I used my favorite yarn and took care to darn in the ends so they wouldn't come loose on you. But I have a confession: All the while, I lived with the quiet, underlying fear that you might not actually show up, that this sweater would remain empty.

I'm so glad you did. I hope you like it.